主 编
张 嘉 妹

摄影：任超 梁鉴 李肖 孟嗣徽 ｜ 撰稿：段晴 范晶晶 李肖 孟嗣徽 张嘉妹 ｜ 特约编辑：颜竹

GANDHARA'S SMILE

THE TOUR OF CULTURAL RELICS IN PAKISTAN

犍陀罗的微笑

巴基斯坦古迹文物巡礼

北京大学外国语学院、东方文学研究中心、巴基斯坦驻中国大使馆

上海三联书店

鸣谢

北京大学加强基础研究专项
"中国文化对外传播的历史影响与
定量研究"资助

教育部人文社会科学重点研究基地
北京大学东方文学研究中心
部分出版资助

犍陀罗的微笑

巴基斯坦古迹文物巡礼

FOREWORD BY AMBASSADOR

序言

I am delighted that publication of "*Gandhara's Smile*", authored by renowned Chinese scholars and experts after their visit to various archaeological sites of ancient Gandhara civilisation of Pakistan, is now a reality.

I congratulate all experts and photographers for their untiring efforts to turn their pilgrimage to Gandhara into an authoritative account about its history, art and architecture. I am confident that this work would spearhead the academic debate in China on ancient history of Pakistan and inspire more such scholarly expeditions in future.

The ancient Gandhara civilization left indelible footprints in the realm of art, architecture, culture and spirituality. Under patronage of Buddhist rulers, the civilization flourished from 1st century B.C. to 7th century A.D. in greater part of Punjab and Khyber Pakhtunkhwa provinces of Pakistan.

The most enduring feature of Gandhara is manifested in its art which mesmerized the world with its artistic brilliance, innovation and intense devotion. The central figure of Gandhara is Lord Buddha, his odyssey for pursuit of knowledge and wisdom, and his message of peace and harmony. Perhaps it was the first experience in history that a spiritual philosophy stirred human's imagination to unleash world's most profound artistic movement.

Besides introducing Buddhism to ancient China and the greater part of East Asia, Gandhara also made a rich contribution to embellish the rich cultural tapestry of modern Pakistan. As the birthplace of Gandhara civilisation, Pakistan has retained many of its traits reflected in progressive and pluralistic outlook.

由中国知名学者专家撰写的《犍陀罗的微笑》一书，在他们探访巴基斯坦古犍陀罗文明考古遗址后于今付梓，我万分欣喜。

参与探访活动的专家、摄影师尽心竭力，将他们的犍陀罗之旅笔耕入文，呈献了这部涉及历史、艺术以及建筑的权威之作，对此，我向他们表示祝贺。我相信这部著作在中国不仅会带动关于研究巴基斯坦古代历史的学术讨论，而且在今后会引发更多此类的学术考察活动。

古代犍陀罗文明在人类艺术、建筑、文化和精神领域都留下了不可磨灭的印迹。公元前1世纪到公元7世纪，犍陀罗文明在信仰佛教的统治者的庇护下，于现今巴基斯坦旁遮普省和开伯尔-普赫图赫瓦省的大部分地区尽显郁勃之气。

犍陀罗文明之不朽之容蕴于其艺术表现中，以其风雅、匠心、奉献等特征令世界为之着迷。犍陀罗艺术表现的核心人物是佛陀，既展现了释迦牟尼追求知识与智慧的艰辛旅程，也传达出他所主张的和平与和谐之理念。那也许是创历史先河之旅，在哲思中被激发了想象力的人类，开启了世界上一场最深刻的艺术运动。

在将佛教传入古代中国和东亚的大部分地区的同时，犍陀罗文明还为当代巴基斯坦的锦绣文化增添了浓墨重彩的一笔。作为犍陀罗文明的发源地，巴基斯坦在多元化的发展历程中保留了该文明的特征。

犍陀罗的微笑

巴基斯坦古迹文物巡礼

Gandhara civilisation must also be credited with the establishment of early linkages between Pakistan and China. Many Chinese monks including Fa Xian and Xuan Zang braved the treacherous mountains and scorching deserts to arrive at the famous Buddhist seminaries in Pakistan. They carried back with them not only the light of wisdom and spirituality but also the warm sentiments of brotherly love and respect which underlies our present fraternal ties.

Year 2021 is a special year when Pakistan and China are celebrating 70th anniversary of establishment of our diplomatic ties. It is also an opportune moment to celebrate the achievements of ancient Gandhara civilisation as the common heritage of our two countries. The best way of paying our tribute could be to continue further research into Gandhara civilisation and unravel its secrets still shrouded in the mystery of time.

Embassy of Pakistan's would keep extending its complete support and assistance in continuing this march of exploration and discovery.

Moin-ul-Haque
Ambassador of Pakistan

犍陀罗文明还见证了巴基斯坦与中国早期往来联系的建立。包括法显、玄奘在内的许多中国高僧,攀越险峻高山,跋涉炎炎沙漠,礼拜巴基斯坦地区的著名佛教圣地。他们带回的不仅是智慧与灵性的光芒,还有手足之爱与敬的温情,这正是如今我们两国间兄弟般情谊的根基所在。

2021 年是一个特殊的年份,这一年巴基斯坦和中国将迎来建交 70 周年的纪念庆典;这也是一个良机,古犍陀罗文明作为我们共同的遗产,两国将庆祝在这一领域(相互合作)所取得的成就。继续进一步研究犍陀罗文明,揭开它那些仍然笼罩在岁月迷雾中的秘密,便是我们最好的献礼。

巴基斯坦大使馆将继续提供全面的支持和帮助,以推动这一探索与发现的进程。

莫因 · 哈克
巴基斯坦驻华大使

(张嘉妹 译)

CONTENTS

FOREWORD BY AMBASSADOR —————————— iii

序言

目录

犍 陀 罗 的 微 笑

巴 基 斯 坦 古 迹 文 物 巡 礼

PREFACE

前言

Pakistan and China are friends and neighbours. We have a long history of cultural exchanges which have been strengthened over a thousand years, and now we have an "All Weather Strategic Cooperative Partnership". At the same time, the high mountains separating us make us mysterious and different from each other.

Along with rapid development over the years, the two nations are experiencing a challenging present and a promising future.

As the flagship project of the "Belt and Road" Initiative, the China-Pakistan Economic Corridor project was officially launched in 2013. As a consequence, the people of both countries are frequently interacting with each other. Our mission now is to understand each other better in order to make this long-term cooperation more successful and prosperous for the peoples of both countries.

To fulfill our mission each one of us is grateful and honored to play a special role to present an amazing Pakistan through its long and multicultural history.

With the strong support of Pakistan Embassy in China, an 8-member delegation consisting of scholars, researchers, experts and photographers from Peking University, Renmin University of China, the Palace Museum of China, kicked off a Gandhara trip in April 2018 to Taxila and Peshawar, the holy land in Pakistan.

Zhang Jiamei

携手前行的路上
更欲知晓你从何而来

高山急流的阻隔，让我们相依而居，却因缺少对彼此的了解而略显神秘。由于经济发展的需要，大多数中国人举目向东，望穿太平洋，对独占鳌头的北美"新大陆"心驰神往。由于历史上的纠葛和近代工业革命下欧洲经济文明的吸引力，大多数操着同属印欧语系语言的巴基斯坦朋友，自然与西面的伊斯兰世界和欧洲国家交流上更少障碍，理念上更多互通。伴随着 2013 年中巴经济走廊项目的正式启动，作为"一带一路"倡议中的旗舰项目，两国人民无论初衷如何，都要面对彼此之间沟通往来日益频繁的现实状况。学习彼此现当代的语言，了解彼此独立发展的过往，关注历史上物质、文化交流往来中相互产生的影响，是我们这些从事与该领域相关的研究人员不可忽视的课题，也是时代赋予我们的不可抗拒的使命。

在巴基斯坦驻中国大使馆一贯强有力的支持下，来自北京大学、中国人民大学、故宫博物院的学者、专家、特邀摄影师等一行 8 人，于 2018 年 4 月踏上了巴基斯坦这片圣洁的土地，开启了犍陀罗文化之旅的第一站行程——塔克西拉和白沙瓦。

巴基斯坦的 4 月是全年最好的季节，温度适中，湿度适中，期待我们彼此的了解，有朝一日也可以如此的"适中"。

VISIT TO UNIVERSITIES AND INSTITUTES

犍陀罗文化之旅 启程 2018

Meticulous arrangements were made for our visit by the Ministry of Foreign Affairs of Pakistan and its Embassy in China. During the 6 days of our stay in Pakistan, we visited Taxila Museum and surrounding sites including Jaulian Buddhist Relics, Sirkap Ancient City Ruins, Bhir Mound Ruins of ancient city, Dharmarajika Stupa and Monastery. We also visited the Peshawar Museum and Buddhist site of Takht-i-Bahi in Mardan. During our visit, we also had discussions with local universities and research institutions which provided a good channel for our future cooperation and research.

We started our travels with the visit to Quaid-e-Azam University, Islamabad, which was our second visit to this prestigious university since 2013. We had an informal discussion with the Dean of Social Science Department and the scholars of History department. Thereafter, Professor Duan Qing and Professor Li Xiao gave lectures at the National Institute of Asian Civilization. Finally, we had an in-depth discussion with the researchers and faculty of the National Institute of Historical and Cultural Research of the university. In the afternoon, our group was invited to visit the Institute of Strategic Studies, Islamabad, and we enjoyed talking with Pakistani experts who know China well.

在巴基斯坦驻中国大使馆的鼎力协助、巴基斯坦外交部周到细致的安排下，在短短6天马不停蹄的行程中，我们一行人实地考察了塔克西拉博物馆及其周边遗址：焦利安佛教遗址、西尔卡普古城遗址、皮尔邱德古城遗址、法王塔遗址等，以及白沙瓦博物馆和附近位于马尔丹的达赫德巴依佛教遗址。当然，在野外考察期间，与当地高校和研究机构的座谈交流是最令人印象深刻的一部分，也为我们今后的合作研究搭建了良好的桥梁。

自 2013 年起，这已经是第二次造访真纳大学了。学校安排得周到全面。我们首先与社会科学部部长及相关系、所学者座谈。继而来到亚洲文明塔克西拉研究所，段晴教授和李肖教授分别做了主题讲座。最后，乘车来到学校的历史文化国立研究所，与科研人员进行了深入交流。下午，我们一行受邀造访巴基斯坦国家战略研究所，与了解中国的巴基斯坦专家相谈甚欢。

We also had the opportunity to visit Peshawar University where we enjoyed an informal discussion with Vice President Professor Mohammad Abid Khan, Director of China Studies Center Professor Zahid Anwar, and distinguished scholars. Then we were invited to visit the Folk Culture Museum and China Studies Center in the campus. This was our first official visit to the Peshawar University which was founded in 1950. Its construction style combines British colonial and local architecture. It was raining the day when we visited and the university appeared particularly attractive in the drizzle.

We hope this kind of communication never stops and flows like a stream and shines like a star.

Zhang Jiamei

有幸正式造访白沙瓦大学,这是第一次。我们与副校长穆罕默德·阿比德·汗教授、中国研究中心主任扎西德·安瓦尔教授及相关院系学者座谈交流,随后参观了校内的民俗博物馆和中国研究中心。白沙瓦大学创建于上世纪 50 年代,结合了本地与英殖民风格的建筑,在蒙蒙细雨中,格外动人。

希望这样的交流能够细水长流,成为了解彼此的众多窗口中,永远亮着灯的那一个。

张嘉妹

在真纳大学亚洲文明塔克西拉研究所
与师生交流

摄影 任超

With teachers and students at Taxila
Institute of Asian Civilization,
Quaid-e-Azam University

Photographed by Ren Chao

李肖教授在真纳大学亚洲文明塔克西
拉研究所做主题发言，张嘉妹副教授
做乌尔都语翻译

摄影 孟嗣徽

Professor Li Xiao giving keynote speech
at Taxila Institute of Asian Civilization,
Quaid-e-Azam University

Photographed by Meng Sihui

犍陀罗的微笑

巴基斯坦古迹文物巡礼

造访白沙瓦大学

摄影 梁鉴

With the Professors at Peshawar University

Photographed by Liang Jian

考察白沙瓦博物馆

摄影 任超

Visiting the Peshawar Museum

Photographed by Ren Chao

考察西尔卡普遗址

摄影 任超

Visiting Sirkap

Photographed by Ren Chao

01

TAXILA

塔克西拉

The history of the ancient Taxila city can be traced back to the Neolithic age, with some sites dating back to 3360 B.C.. The remains of early Indus Valley Civilization have also been excavated here, belonging to the early Harappan Civilization from 2900 B.C..

According to archaeological excavations of artefacts, the ancient Taxila city had become one of the centers of local commerce by around 900 B.C.. During the period of the sixteen ancient kingdoms in north and central parts of the subcontinent, Taxila became the capital of Gandhara and one of the eight commercial centers connected with other cities by 600 B.C.. As Gandhara region changed with the march of Alexander the Great in the 4th century B.C., the capital city had moved to Puskaravati (now Charsadda). Due to frequent warfare within the region, Taxila and other ancient cities gradually formed independent city-states which interacted with other city-states. Several hundred years later when eminent Buddhist monks such as Fa Xian and Xuan Zang traveled to the region, it was called "Taxila State".

In 326 B.C., Alexander the Great marched eastward into the Subcontinent, and from then onwards the wealth of this region became known to the West. When the Mauryan dynasty was established, the founder Chandragupta made Taxila his capital. It is also said that when Ashoka was the prince, he served as governor of the area, so Buddhism may have been introduced to this region at that time. According to the holy monk Xuan Zang's (602-664) *Buddhist Records of the Western World*,

"The kingdom of Ta-ch'a-shi-lo is about 2000 li in circuit, and the capital is about 10 li in circuit. The royal family is extinct and the nobles contend for power by force. Formerly this country was in subjugation to Kapisa, but later it had become a tributary to Kia-shi-mi-lo(Kashmir). The land is renowned for its fertility and produces rich harvests. It is full of streams and fountains. Flowers and fruits are abundant. The climate is temperate. The people are lively and courageous, and they honour the three gems. Although there are many sangharamas, they have become ruinous and deserted, and there are very few priests; and those that are, study the Great Vehicle."(Translated by Samuel Beal, London,1884)

塔克西拉古城的历史可以追溯到新石器时代，据考一些遗址的年代为公元前 3360 年。早期印度河流域城市文明的遗址在此也有发掘，属于早期哈拉帕文明时期，年代大约在公元前 2900 年。

依据考古发掘的器物，至公元前 900 年左右，塔克西拉古城已经成为当地商贸往来的中心之一。公元前 6 世纪，南亚次大陆十六国时期，塔克西拉古城是南亚次大陆八大商业中心之一，犍陀罗国的首都。随着犍陀罗国地域范围的变化，至公元前 4 世纪亚历山大大帝东征至此时，都城已迁至布色羯逻伐底（今开伯尔 - 普赫·图赫瓦省加尔色达市）。在后来连续不断的地区政权纷争中，塔克西拉与其他一些古城逐渐形成独立的城邦格局模式，与其他城邦保持着畅通的交通。当法显、玄奘等高僧几百年后游至此地时，称其为"竺刹尸罗国"。

公元前 326 年，亚历山大帝东征至此，其富裕景况由此为西方所知晓。孔雀王朝建立时期，信奉耆那教的创立者旃陀罗·笈多（月护王）将塔克西拉设为都城。又相传阿育王为太子时，曾任此地总督，故佛教在当时可能已经传入。依高僧玄奘的《大唐西域记》卷三所载，"呾叉始罗国，周二千余里，国大都城周十余里。酋豪力竞，王族绝嗣，往者役属迦毕试国，近又附庸迦湿弥罗国。地称沃壤，稼穑殷盛，泉流多，花果茂。气序和畅，风俗轻勇，崇敬三宝。伽蓝虽多，荒芜已甚，僧徒寡少，并学大乘"。

In 2nd century B.C., the ancient Taxila city became a dependency of the India-Greek Kingdom of Bactria, and a new capital named Sirkap was built near Taxila. From 1st century B.C. to 1st century A.D., the King of India-Scythian built a mint here. Around 20 B.C., Gondophares I, the founder of the India-Parthian Kingdom, conquered the region and made Taxila its capital.

This place has been famous since ancient times for the dissemination of advanced knowledge. According to Jātakas in Pali language, prince Brahmadatta and others had been studying here. It is said that the famous grammarian Panini got educated here, and Kauṭilya, the advisor of Chandragupta Maurya, had taught at the university in Taxila. Although the "university" here is quite different from today's university model, it is regarded as one of the earliest universities in the world. When Ashoka succeeded the throne, Taxila became a shrine for teaching Buddhism.

The archaeological site of the ancient city of Taxila was excavated in 1913, by John Marshall (1876-1958), the director of the Archaeological Survey of India. The site is located 35 km northwest from Rawalpindi and belongs to the present city of Taxila. During our visit, we had the honor to visit Taxila Museum, Jaulian Buddhist Relics, Sirkap Ancient City Ruins, Bhir Mound Ruins of ancient city, Dharmarajika Stupa and Monastery, etc.

Zhang Jiamei

公元前 2 世纪，塔克西拉古城成为巴克特里亚印度 - 希腊王国的属地，新君主在其附近，隔岸建起了新都城——西尔卡普。公元前 1 世纪至公元 1 世纪，印度 - 斯基泰国王在这里兴建了铸币厂。

大约公元前 20 年，印度 - 安息王国的创建者冈多帕莱斯一世征服该地，并将塔克西拉作为都城。

另外，自古以来，此地便以高等知识传播地而闻名。在巴利语本生故事及其注释，曾记述梵授王等人来此研学。相传文法家波你尼及大医耆婆亦曾于此地受业。据传，孔雀王朝开国君主旃陀罗笈多的国师考底利耶曾在塔克西拉讲学。这里的"学校"虽然与如今的"大学"模式大相径庭，但从某种意义上，已被视为世界上最早的"大学"之一。当孔雀王朝第三世君王阿育王继位后，这里成为传授学习佛学的圣地。

塔克西拉古城的考古遗址，位于今拉瓦尔品第市西北 35 公里处，属今塔克西拉市。该遗址首次挖掘于 1913 年，时任印度考古局局长马歇尔领队。我们此行有幸考察了塔克西拉博物馆、焦利安佛教遗址、西尔卡普古城遗址、皮尔邱德古城遗址、法王塔等。

张嘉妹

SIKRAP

西尔卡普

Sirkap is located near Taxila in Punjab province of today's Pakistan. The city was built by Graeco-Bactrian King Demetrius around 180 B.C.. The city was rebuilt during the time of Menander. The site was excavated twice in 1912-1930 and 1944-1945. According to the comparison of photographs from different periods of excavation, the site has been repaired several times.

The site of Sirkap presents a Greek-style network of city-states. The layout of the city revolves around a main road, with 15 streets perpendicular to the main road. Some scholars say that the city's design is similar to that of Macedonia's Olynthus. A large number of Greek-style artefacts have been excavated here, especially the coins engraved with Graeco–Bactrian Kings. Of course, the local characteristics are displayed in details. It is said that the city had been rebuilt after the Scythian's invasion. After an earthquake in 30 A.D., the Parthian renovated the city and built "Double-headed Eagle Tower" and "Sun Temple" etc. Later, the city became a part of the Kushan Empire, but during this time the city was abandoned and a new city, Sirsukh, was built 1.5km to the North-East. Greek decorative elements can be found in the Buddhist Stupas excavated in Sirkap. Under influence of Bactria, the interaction and integration between different religions and cultures can also be found reflected in various Greek-style architectures here.

Zhang Jiamei

西尔卡普在现今巴基斯坦旁遮普省塔克西拉附近，据考于公元前 180 年左右由希腊 - 巴克特里亚王德米特里乌斯兴建，据说在弥兰陀（米兰德）一世时重建。该遗址先后于 1912～1930 年、1944～1945 年经过两次挖掘，呈现出今日遗址的结构面貌。据挖掘后不同时期照片的对比，可发现其细部也曾几经修缮。

西尔卡普遗址呈现了希腊式的网格式城邦布局。建筑布局围绕一条主干道展开，15 条街道与主干道垂直交叉。学者认为该城市的设计类似马其顿的奥林索斯。曾经在这里发掘出大量希腊风格的手工制品，尤其是刻有希腊 - 巴克特里亚王的钱币和代表希腊神话场景的石板。当然，在细节装饰上，自然呈现出本土特色。据说，斯基泰人入侵该地时，重建了此城。在公元 30 年的一次大地震后，安息人又修缮了这里，并新建了"双头鹰塔"、"太阳神庙"等建筑。再后，该地成为贵霜帝国的一部分，但在此时期，该城遭到遗弃，并在其东北方 1.5 公里处帝国兴建了新城西尔苏克。在西尔卡普发掘的佛塔中，可以发现希腊式的装饰元素。在巴克特里亚管辖或影响下的近两个世纪中，宗教文化间的互动与融合也体现在带有希腊色彩的各式建筑中。

张嘉妹

古城街道

摄影 任超

Sirkap

Photographed by Ren Chao

古城房屋遗址

摄影 任超

Streets of old city in Sirkap

Photographed by Ren Chao

犍陀罗的微笑

巴基斯坦古迹文物巡礼

两位教授在西尔卡普遗址考察地层，遗址最底层属希腊时期

摄影 任超

Professors at the site of Sirkap

Photographed by Ren Chao

塔遗址

摄影 任超

Tower site

Photographed by Ren Chao

双头鹰塔遗址

摄影 任超

The ruins of Double-headed Eagle Tower

Photographed by Ren Chao

太阳神庙遗址

摄影 任超

Sun Temple site

Photographed by Ren Chao

BHIR MOUND

皮尔邝德

Bhir Mound is located near present-day Taxila city in Punjab of Pakistan, along with other cities excavated in the surroundings, constitutes the "Taxila relic" which was listed in the world heritage site by UNESCO in 1980. Some of the oldest ruins ever found in the ancient city of Taxila can be traced back to 6th century B.C.. The site was excavated five times, which respectively took place in 1913-1925, 1944-1945, 1966-1967, 1998-2000, and 2002.

According to the present excavations, the lowest and oldest layer is from the 6th to 5th century B.C., when it was one of the administrative regions of the eastern-most part of the Achaemenid Dynasty of Persia. The second layer, which began in the 4th century B.C., existed during Alexander the Great's eastward march; then the third layer dates back to the 3rd century B.C. from the period of the Maurya dynasty; and the fourth and uppermost layer belongs to the era after the Maurya dynasty.

In 518 B.C., Darius I of Achaemenid conquered the region and incorporated Taxila into the Persian Empire as an administrative province in its eastern part. In 326 B.C., when Alexander the Great marched eastward to this region, the Raja surrendered without fighting. Following the retreat of the Greek army and the establishment of the Maurya Dynasty, Buddhism flourished in Taxila during the reign of Emperor Ashoka. In 184 B.C., Bactria invaded and occupied the region, and the Greek King Demetrius began his rule here.

Zhang Jiamei

位于今日巴基斯坦旁遮普省塔克西拉附近，与周边挖掘出的其他遗址一起，共同构成的"塔克西拉遗迹"，于 1980 年被联合国教文组织列入世界遗产名录。在这里，可探寻到迄今为止塔克西拉古城最古老的部分废墟遗址，时间可追溯到公元前 6 世纪。遗址先后于 1913 年 ~ 1925 年、1944 年 ~ 1945 年、1966 年 ~ 1967 年、1998 年 ~ 2000 年、2002 年 5 次被挖掘。

从目前的挖掘状况看，最下面最古老的一层据考证属于公元前 6 至前 5 世纪，当时此地属于波斯阿契美尼德王朝最东部的行政区域；往上即第二层始于公元前 4 世纪，存在于亚历山大大帝东征时期；再向上第三层始于公元前 3 世纪，孔雀王朝时期；第四层也是最上面一层，属于孔雀王朝之后的年代。

公元前 518 年，波斯阿契美尼德王朝的大流士一世征服该地区，将塔克西拉地区纳入波斯帝国东部的一个行政省内。公元前 326 年亚历山大大帝东征至此时，该地的王公不战而降。接下来伴随希腊军队的撤退和孔雀王朝的建立，到第三任君主阿育王时期，佛教盛行于此地。公元前 184 年，巴克特里亚入侵并占据该地区，希腊王德米特里进驻并治理此地。

张嘉妹

犍陀罗的微笑 巴基斯坦古迹文物巡礼

房屋遗址

摄影 任超

House sites at Bhir Mound

Photographed by Ren Chao

子城遗址

摄影 任超

The South-east corner of the city at Bhir Mound

Photographed by Ren Chao

古井遗址

摄影 任超

Well site at Bhir Mound

Photographed by Ren Chao

DHARMARAJIKA STUPA

———

法王塔

Dharmarajika stupa, along with the large monastic complex, is also called "Chir Tope". It is located at Taxila, Punjab province, Pakistan, which is the central area of ancient Gandhara Buddhist art. The stupa is the largest and the most remarkable stupa remains of Taxila. In 1860s, Sir Alexander Cunningham affirmed that nothing was left of its outer casting after his investigation of the earth's surface of the stupa. At the beginning of 20th century, Sir John Marshall excavated the base of the stupa, and brought to light a large number of other interesting structures, which included stupas and monastic quarters.

法王塔亦称"基尔佛塔"，位于今天巴基斯坦旁遮普省塔克西拉境内，是古代犍陀罗佛教艺术的中心地区之一。该塔为塔克西拉境内地面上最大、最醒目的佛塔遗迹。

早在 19 世纪 60 年代，康宁汉爵士对这座佛塔遗迹地表以上部分进行了调查，得出了此佛塔即是古代佛寺的中心，其周围也没有其他附属遗存的结论。

20 世纪初马歇尔爵士对大塔周围进行了发掘，发现大量环绕大塔而时代较晚的小窣堵波和佛寺建筑遗迹，更正并充实了康宁汉的结论。

The archaeological site of Dharmarajika has a stupa and monastic site. Judging from the style of the shape of the dome and the whole stupa, it was founded in Maurya dynasty (around 324 B.C. - 188 B.C.), around 2nd century B.C., and underwent an expansion in 4th century CE. There are relics of original railings around the circumambulatory path, which are similar to Sanchi stupa in Central India, indicating that the style of this stupa is generally same as Sanchi stupa.

Dharmarajika stupa is a typical stupa before Kushan Empire (45–250). The dome is almost semi-circular, being same as the traditional style of stupas in Central India. It is the earliest great stupa in Gandhara area. It was likely to have been built for Ashoka to house and worship the relics of the Buddha Shakyamuni, and was abandoned in 6th century.

The base of the stupa is masonry structure. It is circular in plan with stairways on crossed axes, 46 meters in diameter. It is just the structure recorded in *the Vinaya of Mahāsaṃghikas*, chapter 33, "At that time, Buddha has made the stupa of Kāśyapa Buddha by himself. The stupa has a square base, railings around it, two-storey platforms and projected landings in four directions. On the stupa stands a pinnacle, to which several disks are connected." The projected landings in four directions refers to the platforms where stairways connected the base and the circumambulatory path on crossed axes. The body of the dome is filled with earth and stone, and the surface is of masonry construction. Beside the east projected part, there are some other remains. All of them are niches of sitting Buddhas. The niches with segmental trapezoidal arch and trefoil arch are alternatively arranged. They're supposed to be reliefs during Gandharan period. The masonry base under the dome is arranged in radial pattern. The dome collapsed, but the height of the remaining part still reaches to 15 meters. The majestic scale of the stupa is remarkable.

法王塔寺院包含有覆钵型窣堵波和僧院建筑，由其覆钵丘塔体推测，大约始建于公元前 2 世纪印度孔雀王朝（约公元前 324 年～约前 188 年）时期，公元 4 世纪又进行扩建。佛塔环形礼拜道周边尚存始建时期与印度中部桑奇大塔相同的栏楯遗迹，可以推断此塔的形制基本与桑奇大塔相同。法王塔属于典型的贵霜王朝（45 年～ 250 年）之前的覆钵型佛塔，塔身较低矮，呈覆丘状，为印度中部窣堵波的传统样式，该塔应是犍陀罗地区最早的大塔，可能为阿育王供奉释迦牟尼佛真身舍利而建，废弃于公元 6 世纪。佛塔基坛为圆形，以石砌成，直径 46 米，东南西北四面有长方形平台，为《摩诃僧祇律》记载覆钵塔的结构："尔时世尊自起迦叶佛塔，下基四方，周匝栏楯，圆起二重，方牙四出。上施盘盖，长表轮相。"所谓的"方牙四出"就是基坛四面的长方形平台，有踏步从环形礼拜道上到这个和基坛相连的"方牙"之上。塔体积土石为覆钵形，外砌石块，在东侧"方牙"所邻塔壁上有残存的塔身饰板浮雕，均为坐佛的佛龛，有梯形和双拱形两种，间隔排列，应为犍陀罗时期后加装饰浮雕构件。覆钵之下的台基有轮辐状石砌结构。覆钵部现已部分坍塌，但残存部分仍高约 15 米，可以想见当年的雄姿和规模。这座大窣堵波四周矗立着四座体现犍陀罗艺术风格不同发展阶段特点的寺院和若干个陆续增建的还愿窣堵波。这些建筑最初布局协调合理，其后随着数量骤增而变得杂乱无序，挤满了全部可用的空间。

Around the great stupa, there are four monasteries and several votive stupas. The styles of the monasteries are showing different stages of Gandhara art. The layout of the whole building complex was first organized, then gradually went to a disarrayed way with the increase of constructions, and finally filled up the space. The excavation works around the stupa have also brought out precious cultural relics, such as the relics of Buddha, silver scrolls engraved with the name of Taxila.

Gandhara Buddhist complexes are usually composed of a stupa courtyard and a monastery. Some people think this kind of complex is the most important innovation of Gandhara Buddhist architecture. The pattern has spread from Gandhara to Afghanistan and Central Asia, then to Tarim Basin and Central China, and even influenced East Asia.

Li Xiao

该窣堵波旁边的遗迹内还曾发掘出佛舍利、镌有塔克西拉名称的银牒等珍贵文物。

犍陀罗地区佛寺的基本组合由供奉窣堵波的塔院及供僧众们修行的僧院两部分组成，有观点认为这是犍陀罗佛教建筑最重要的创新，且这种模式从犍陀罗地区向西扩展到阿富汗和中亚地区，最后进入塔里木盆地直至中原和东亚地区。

李肖

犍陀罗的微笑

巴基斯坦古迹文物巡礼

寺院航拍图

摄影 任超

Aerial view of Dharmarajika Stupa complex

Photographed by Ren Chao

法王塔

摄影 梁鉴

Dharmarajika Stupa

Photographed by Liang Jian

犍
陀
罗
的
微
笑

巴
基
斯
坦
古
迹
文
物
巡
礼

环形礼拜道上残存的石栏楯遗迹

摄影 李肖

Relics of the original railings around
the circumambulatory path

Photographed by Li Xiao

从地面上到佛塔"方牙"和基坛的踏步

摄影 李肖

The projected platform and stairways
connected the base and the circumambulatory
path

Photographed by Li Xiao

塔身饰板佛龛

摄影 李肖

Niches around the drum of the stupa

Photographed by Li Xiao

JAULIAN

焦利安

The area of Gandhara is renowned for the number of surviving numerous Buddha images, more than those in Central Asia and India. It is even possibly the hometown of a thousand Buddhas of the *bhadrakalpa*, especially when we take notice that the *Bhadrakalpika-sūtra* which propagated the thought of a thousand Buddhas of the *bhadrakalpa* was probably compiled in this area. The main schemes for the stupa decorations at the Jaulian Monastery might include the Buddhas of the Three Times, the first five Buddhas in the *bhadrakalpa*, the twenty-five Buddhas in the *Buddhavamsa*, etc.

The Jaulian Buddhist complex consists of a vihara court and a large stupa court. The vihara court lies in the west of the whole site, covering more than half of the site while the stupa court in the east is divided into two parts by two platforms of different heights. The lower north part is linked to a small square court in the west. The main stupa stands in the center of the south higher part. There exist many redeeming stupas and shrines densely built around the stupa and steps; around the stupa courtyard are large shrines. The vihara court in the west is a two-storey architecture with an open yard and a central pool; it is also equipped with drainage culverts, indoor lamp shrines, slate roads and step facilities. An ordination hall (prāsāda), a dining hall, a kitchen, a warehouse, and a toilet are also included.

Li Xiao，Fan Jingjing

犍陀罗地区以现存数量众多的佛像而闻名，远胜于中亚与中印度。此地甚至可能就是贤劫千佛的故乡，尤其是当我们考虑到：宣扬贤劫千佛思想的《贤劫经》很可能就诞生于此地。焦利安佛塔上装饰的佛像主题或许包括了三世佛、贤劫最初的五佛、《佛陀世系》中的二十五佛等。

焦利安佛寺由一个僧院和一座大型塔院构成。僧院位于佛寺西侧，占据了整个寺院的一半以上。塔院位于僧院东侧，内部由两个高度不同的平台分成南北高低两院，北侧低院西边尚有一个较小的方院与之衔接。主塔即位于南侧高院中央，周边和踏道两侧及前部密布还愿小塔、龛像等；塔院周匝建置高大佛龛。西侧僧院为两层建筑，庭院、中央水池，排水暗渠、室内的灯龛、佛龛、经行石路及楼梯俱备，说戒堂、食堂、厨、仓、厕等设施完善。

李肖，范晶晶

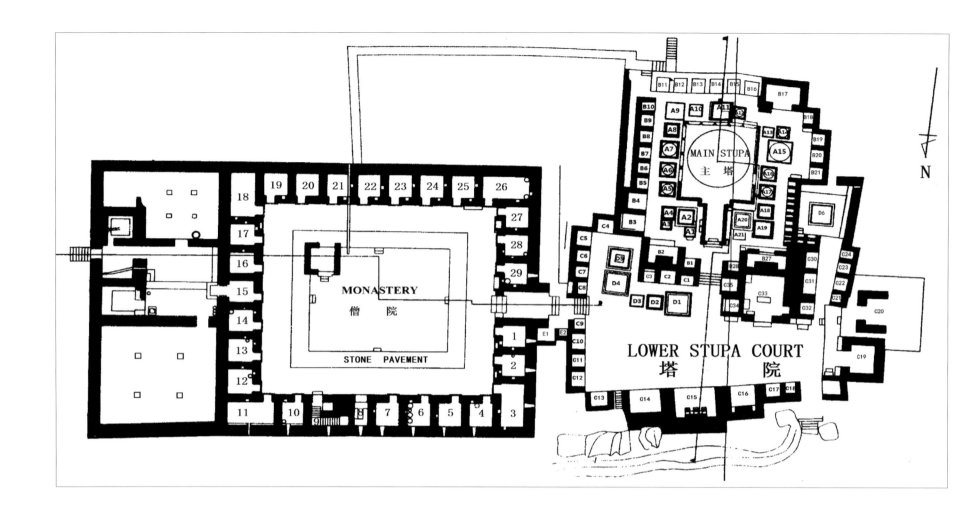

焦利安佛寺平面图

Plan of Jaulian Stupa and Monastery

主塔顶部遗存

摄影 梁鉴

Remains of the top of the Main Stupa

Photographed by Liang Jian

主塔踏道及北面

摄影 梁鉴

Steps of the Main Stupa and
the North Wall

Photographed by Liang Jian

禅定佛像
公元 4~5 世纪，位于主塔南面，灰泥，
塔克西拉博物馆（左图）

摄影 任超

Buddha in meditation,
4th-5th century, on the south wall of the Main Stupa, Jaulian,
clay, Taxila Museum

Photographed by Ren Chao

禅定佛像细部（右图）

摄影 任超

Buddha in meditation detail

Photographed by Ren Chao

GANDHARA'S SMILE
THE TOUR OF CULTURAL RELICS IN PAKISTAN

主塔南侧大佛像及还愿塔
公元 4~5 世纪

摄影　梁鉴

The south wall of the Main Stupa and the
redeeming stupa, 4th-5th century

Photographed by Liang Jian

 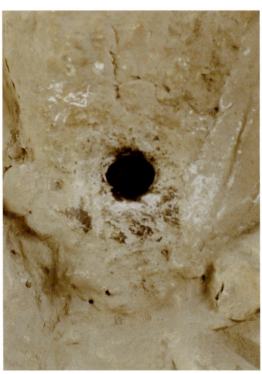

药师佛像
公元 3~4 世纪，位于主塔北面，灰泥，
祈求疗疾者可将手指伸入佛像肚脐处
的小孔。

摄影　任超

Healing Buddha, 3rd-4th century,
on the north wall of the Main Stupa,
Stucco, the hole at the navel was
intended for a suppliant to place his
finger in when offering prayers against
certain bodily ailments.

Photographed by Ren Chao

佛立像遗存
公元 4~5 世纪，位于主塔北面

摄影 梁鉴

Remains of standing Buddhas
4th-5th century, on the north wall of the Main Stupa

Photographed by Liang Jian

犍陀罗的微笑

巴基斯坦古迹文物巡礼

说法佛坐像
位于主塔东面，灰泥

摄影 任超

Seated Buddha in the teaching attitude,
on the pilaster of the east wall of the
Main Stupa, Stucco.

Photographed by Ren Chao

A15 号塔基南面与西面，
2~5 世纪

摄影 梁鉴

View of subsidiary Stupa A15, Jaulian
(showing the south and west sides of the
podium with large sculptures), 2nd-5th
century.

Photographed by Liang Jian

犍
陀
罗
的
微
笑

巴
基
斯
坦
古
迹
文
物
巡
礼

A15 号塔基西面与北面，
2~5 世纪

摄影 梁鉴

View of subsidiary Stupa A15, Jaulian
(showing the west and north sides of the
podium with large sculptures), 2nd-5th
century.

Photographed by Liang Jian

A15 号塔基西面浮雕

摄影 梁鉴

West side of subsidiary stupa A15

Photographed by Liang Jian

A15 号塔基北面浮雕

摄影 梁鉴

North side of subsidiary stupa A15

Photographed by Liang Jian

A11 号塔基东面，公元 4~5 世纪

摄影　任超

East side of subsidiary stupa A11, Jaulian, 4th-5th century.

Photographed by Ren Chao

说法佛坐像
A11 号塔基西面

摄影 梁鉴

Seated Buddha in the teaching attitude,
on the west wall of subsidiary stupa A11

Photographed by Liang Jian

A2 号塔基西面与北面，公元 4 世纪

摄影 梁鉴

View of subsidiary stupa A2, Jaulian
(showing the west and north sides of the
podium), 4th century.

Photographed by Liang Jian

D4 号塔北面
公元 5 世纪

摄影 梁鉴

North side of subsidiary stupa D4
5th century

Photographed by Liang Jian

主塔及环绕小塔

摄影 任超

The main stupa and surrounding votive stupas

Photographed by Ren Chao

焦利安僧舍

摄影 任超

Vihara court at Jaulian

Photographed by Ren Chao

TAXILA MUSEUM

塔克西拉博物馆

The construction of the Taxila Museum started in 1918, and was completed in 1928. Since then the museum has been opened for public. Most of the objects of its collection, especially the Gandhara Buddhist artefacts from the 1st to 7th century, were excavated from the ruins of ancient Taxila. In the closed area of the courtyard, the room where Sir John Marshall used to work and rest still remains, furnished with simple tables, chairs and a bed. In the public exhibition hall, the items on display include Buddha images, pagodas, coins and seals, as if speaking of the life back to about 2000 years ago. Although there display also exhibits of Hindu and Jain relics, as well as tools, jewelry, toys and so on in daily life, Gandhara Buddhist statues are undoubtedly the dominant collection here in terms of quantity, craftsmanship and cultural representation.

Fan Jingjing

塔克西拉博物馆始建于 1918 年，于 1928 年竣工并对外开放。其中大部分馆藏，尤其是公元 1 至 7 世纪的犍陀罗佛教艺术藏品，都来自古城塔克西拉的出土文物。庭院中不对外开放的区域里，还保留着马歇尔爵士曾经工作和休息的房间，里面陈设着简单的桌椅、床铺。公共展厅里陈列着佛像、佛塔、钱币、印章，仿佛在诉说着近两千年前此地的生活。展品中尽管也包括印度教、耆那教的文物，还有日常使用的工具、首饰、玩具等，但无论从数量、工艺还是从文化代表性来看，犍陀罗风格的佛教造像无疑是这里最重要的藏品。

范晶晶

犍陀罗的微笑

巴基斯坦古迹文物巡礼

施无畏印立佛像
公元 2~3 世纪，法王塔

摄影 任超

Standing Buddha in reassuring pose
2nd-3rd century, Dharmarajika

Photographed by Ren Chao

禅定佛像
公元 5 世纪，焦利安，灰泥

摄影 梁鉴

Buddha in meditation,
5th century, Jaulian, stucco

Photographed by Liang Jian

禅定佛像，公元 4~5 世纪，
焦利安，灰泥

摄影 任超

Buddha in meditation,
4th-5th century, Jaulian, Stucco

Photographed by Ren Chao

禅定佛像细部

摄影 梁鉴

Buddha in meditation detail

Photographed by Liang Jian

犍陀罗的微笑

巴基斯坦古迹文物巡礼

佛头像，公元 3~4 世纪，焦利安，灰泥

摄影 梁鉴

Buddha heads, 3rd-4th century, Jaulian

Photographed by Liang Jian

佛头像

摄影 梁鉴

Buddha head detail

Photographed by Liang Jian

犍陀罗的微笑

巴基斯坦古迹文物巡礼

一组佛头像，公元 3~4 世纪，
焦利安，灰泥

摄影 梁鉴

Buddha heads, 3rd-4th century,
Jaulian

Photographed by Liang Jian

佛头像，2~4世纪，焦利安，
灰泥

摄影 任超

Buddha head, 2nd-4th century, Jaulian,
stucco

Photographed by Ren Chao

02

PESHAWAR

白沙瓦

Peshawar surrounded by mountains in the east, west and north, faces the open Punjab plain in the south (southeast). Located at the east end of Khyber Pass, it has played an important role as a commercial hub connecting different regions since Kushan period. The valley of Peshawar was often used by invaders from the west and north as the route into the subcontinent.

The present Peshawar is adjacent to the border between Pakistan and Afghanistan and the most important city connecting Central, South and West Asia. Looking back at the historical Silk Road, and in records of monk Fa Xian and Xuan Zang, the city was always described as a commercial center, a holy land for peoples from all around the world and an ancient city full of different ethnic groups. This leads to a picture, vividly unfolding in our mind, and we wonder which is the true face of this city.

The history of Peshawar can be traced back to 539 B.C.. It is one of the oldest cities in the subcontinent of South Asia. According to a statistic of 2017, the population of the city has reached 1,970,042, which makes it the largest city in Khyber Pakhtunkhwa and the sixth largest city in Pakistan.

There are wide roads and railways. The Grand Trunk Road (GT Road) was built in the 16th century by Sultan Sher Shah, but the connecting line has existed at least for 2000 years. It is one of the oldest and longest roads in Asia. The eastern end of this road is in today's Bangladesh, runs through India, passes through Pakistan's Punjab and Khyber Pakhtunkhwa provinces, and finally reaches the Afghan capital, Kabul.

There are rich historical Buddhist relics here. Kanishka ordered the construction of the world's tallest building at that time—the Kanishka Stupa.

白沙瓦位于广阔的白沙瓦山谷中，东、西、北三面群山环绕，南面（东南）朝向开阔的旁遮普平原。白沙瓦处于开伯尔山口的东端，自贵霜时期起，开伯尔山口便成为南来北往的商道。此前，从西面和北面进入次大陆的入侵者也必经此地。

如今，白沙瓦毗邻巴阿边境，是连通中亚、南亚、西亚的枢纽，南亚次大陆由此通往中东。在对丝绸之路的回溯中，在高僧法显、玄奘传于后世的文字中，在历史学家的记录中，读到"布路沙布逻"、"丈夫宫"、"百花之都"这些称呼时，那个热闹繁华、四通八达的商贸中心，那个让人心驰神往的佛教圣地，那个融入不同族群的历史古城，便会如连绵画卷，栩栩如生地在人们的脑海中缓缓展开。

据文献记载，白沙瓦的历史可以追溯到公元前 539 年，是南亚次大陆可以考证的最古老城市之一。据 2017 年统计数据显示，白沙瓦城市人口已经达到 197 万，是开伯尔 - 普赫图赫瓦省第一大城市，巴基斯坦第六大城市，且白沙瓦大区人口已经达到 427 万。

这里有四通八达的公路和铁路。连接南亚次大陆和中亚地区的大干道，是亚洲最古老最长的公路之一，修建于 16 世纪舍尔沙统治时期，而其连通的路线却有近 2000 年的历史。该路线东端起始于孟加拉国，横穿印度，经巴基斯坦境内旁遮普省、开伯尔 - 普赫图赫瓦省，最终到达阿富汗首都喀布尔。

这里有丰富的历史佛教遗迹。迦腻色伽王下令兴建了当时世界上最高的建筑——大佛塔。

犍陀罗的微笑

巴基斯坦古迹文物巡礼

Peshawar has always been a prominent political position. When Kanishka ascended the throne, he changed the capital from Pushkalavati (near present-day Charsadda) to Purushapura, which, centuries later, the Mughal emperor Akbar the Great named Peshawar . The name is still used today.

In the winter of 327-326 B.C., Alexander the Great marched eastward to India, conquered Peshawar and Swat valley. A few years later Alexander the Great died on the way back, his senior general established the Seleucid Empire, and Peshawar became a part of the administrative region of Seleucus I Nicator. With the establishment of Maurya Dynasty, wars broke out between the two countries. Chandragupta gradually conquered the subcontinent in northwest region, so Peshawar was incorporated into the Maurya imperial territory in 303 B.C..

In 255 B.C., the governor of Bactria, Diodotus I, declared independence. Around 190 B.C., Kabul, Gandhara and Punjab were incorporated into the territory of his Kingdom. Later, the city was ruled by "Iran - Parthians" and then became a part of India. It is said that the eminent Buddhist monastery Takht-i-Bahi was built around 46 A.D. during this period.

In 128 A.D., during the reign of Kanishka, the ancient city of Peshawar became the capital of Kushan Empire. Kanishka had the great Buddhist monastery built, and the Kaniska Stupa was constructed after his death.

Around 260 A.D., Shapur I of Sasanid led his troops to attack Peshawar, destroying Buddhist buildings in the valley, including stupas and monasteries, and controlled the trading port in Peshawar westward. In the early 5th century, the city was occupied by Kidārites from Central Asia.

这里占据突出的政治地位。迦腻色伽王登基后，将都城从布色羯逻伐底城（今加尔色达）迁到了布路沙布逻。莫卧儿王朝阿克巴大帝定其名为白沙瓦，沿用至今。

公元前 327~ 前 326 年冬，亚历山大大帝东征印度，攻下白沙瓦山谷地及附近斯瓦特等地区。几年后亚历山大在东征返途中去世，手下大将塞琉古建帝国，白沙瓦遂成塞琉古一世统辖区域的一部分。接下来，孔雀王朝建立，月护王逐步征服了南亚次大陆西北部地区，将该地区并入孔雀王朝的版图（公元前 303 年）。据希腊历史学家麦加斯梯尼记载，那时，白沙瓦古城是当时连接帝国首都华氏城（今印度比哈尔邦巴特纳附近）的最西端城市。

公元前 255 年，巴克特里亚总督狄奥多图斯一世宣告独立。随着孔雀王朝的衰落，其子德米特里一世即位后，在公元前 190 年左右，将喀布尔、犍陀罗和旁遮普等地纳入王国的版图。之后，在列国的争战中，该城被"伊朗 - 帕提亚"统治过，后在冈多帕莱斯一世时期，并入"印度 - 帕提亚"。据称，公元 46 年，佛教寺院达赫德巴依在附近（今马尔丹）建立。

公元 128 年，迦腻色伽统治时期，白沙瓦古城成为帝国唯一都城。迦腻色伽修建了佛教大寺院。此地兴建的迦腻色伽大塔是宝贵的佛教遗址。

大约公元 260 年，萨珊帝国沙普尔一世率兵进攻白沙瓦，大肆破坏山谷中的佛教建筑，包括大塔、寺院等。不敌萨珊的贵霜王朝走向衰落，自此，萨珊帝国管控了白沙瓦地区西去的商贸口岸。之后，迦腻色伽三世再度夺回整个白沙瓦地区，但在公元 5 世纪初期，该城又被来自中亚的寄多罗王占领。

The Pashtuns arrived in the region in 11th century, and the Dilazak branch settled in Peshawar. According to Massoudi the Arab historian, the region was known as Parashawar in the mid-10th century.

Between 1179 and 1180, Muhammad Ghori captured Peshawar, which was then destroyed by the Mongol army at the beginning of the 13th century. Peshawar was the central city of northwest of the subcontinent during the Lodhi dynasty in the Delhi Sultanate. In the late 15th century, contemporary Yusufzai and Gigyani branches of Pushtun, belonging to Khashi Khel tribe, came to Peshawar area. They fought against Dilazak Pushtun tribe near Mardan in 1515, and the defeated Dilazak tribe moved to the east of the Indus valley.

In 1526, Babur, the founder of the Mughal Dynasty, defeated Taulat Khan of the Lodhi Dynasty and seized Peshawar as a base for further military conquest. But in 1540 the Pashtun Maharaja Sher Shah defeated Humayun of Mughal, and it was during his reign that the famous Grand Trunk Road in the region was constructed, and Peshawar was promoted to a flurishing trade center.

During Aurangzeb's reign, the governor of Kabul, Mohabbat Khan bin Ali Mardan Khan, was appointed to govern Peshawar, and in 1630 he had the famous Mohabbat Khan mosque constructed.

公元 11 世纪，普什图人来到这里，其中迪拉扎克的一支定居下来。据阿拉伯历史学家马苏迪记载，在 10 世纪中期，这一地区以"布罗沙瓦尔"一名而为人知晓。

1179 年至 1180 年间，白沙瓦被阿富汗古尔王朝的穆罕默德·古力攻占，13 世纪初，又毁于蒙古大军的铁蹄之下。在德里苏丹国洛蒂王朝时期，白沙瓦是南亚次大陆西北部地区的中心城市。15 世纪后期，当代普什图人的祖先——优素夫扎伊部和吉格亚尼部——来到白沙瓦附近地区。这两个部（族）的普什图人共属于赫什子部落，他们与之前定居在此地区的迪拉扎克普什图部落于 1515 年在马尔丹附近开战，结果战败的迪拉扎克部落迁移到了印度河流域的东边。

1526 年，莫卧儿王朝的创建者巴布尔击败洛蒂王朝的道拉德汗，夺取白沙瓦，将这里作为进一步军事征服的基地。但巴布尔之子胡马雍继位十年后，于 1540 年被强势崛起的普什图王公舍尔沙·苏利击败，逃亡波斯。16 世纪舍尔沙在白沙瓦地区修建了著名的大干道。这条公路的修建，让白沙瓦成为重要的贸易中心。

到奥朗则布时期，宫廷派往驻守喀布尔的总督穆哈巴德汗在 17 世纪管辖期，将白沙瓦作为喀布尔地区的冬都，并于 1630 年兴建了著名的穆哈巴德汗清真寺。

In British colonial period, the British government introduced western education to Peshawar, setting up local schools. And Edwards College and Islamia College were established in 1901 and 1913 respectively. The British government separated Peshawar and its surrounding areas from Punjab province in 1901 and made Peshawar the capital of the new province, the North-West Frontier Province (present Khyber Pakhtunkhwa province).

After Pakistan was founded in 1947, Peshawar became a cultural center in the northwest. The Peshawar University was established in 1950 and gradually incorporated other research institutions of the British colonial period nearby. Since the 1980s, the influx of refugees completely overwhelmed municipal Peshawar, at the same time greatly changed the demographic here, which in turn affected the social, cultural and political landscape.

As a city connecting the Indian subcontinent and Central Asia, Peshawar has always been thriving as one of the trade hubs with caravans coming and going, and its rich culture, beliefs and thoughts being brought to other areas through merchants.

Zhang Jiamei

据英国探险家威廉姆·默克罗夫特记录，18 世纪后期，白沙瓦依然是连接布哈拉和南亚次大陆的商贸中心。同时，这里还是农业高产区，以及主要干果出口区。英殖民期间，英政府将西式教育引入白沙瓦，在当地设立了隶属于圣公会的教会学校，并分别于 1901 年和 1913 年建立了爱德华兹学院和伊斯兰学院。为了更好地治理本地，英政府于 1901 年将白沙瓦及其周边地区从旁遮普分离出来，并立白沙瓦为新省份，即西北边境省的首府。

1947 年巴基斯坦建国后，白沙瓦成为西北部地区的文化中心。1950 年，建立白沙瓦大学，逐渐将英殖民时期的研究机构并入其中。上世纪 80 年代后，难民的涌入完全超出了白沙瓦市政的承受力，甚至改变了人口构成，影响了社会文化面貌以及政治动向。

在连接南亚次大陆和中亚的商道上，白沙瓦始终是南来北往的中心枢纽，往来的商队让白沙瓦地区很难归于平静。从这里，奇闻怪谈、各派思想和商品货物一起，跟随商贾小贩传往各地。

张嘉妹

TAKHT-I-BAHI

达赫德巴依

Takht-i-Bahi is situated in the center of ancient Gandhara area with its relevant remains extending on the north slope of a high mountain range, covering an area about 1.5 kilometers from east to west. The most important architectural legacy lies in the easternmost area, on three broad ridges, which are running high in south and low in north. The main architecture is constructed on the central and most spacious ridge of the three.

In 1871, F.H. Wilcher headed the dig of a part of Buddhist sites in Takht-i-Bahi; in 1875, A. Cunningham published his detailed report of his investigation of the remains; from 1907 to 1908, D.B. Sponner conducted a systematic archaeological excavation of Takht-i-Bahi; H. Hargreaves further cleaned up the remains between 1901 and 1911. According to scholars, the sites of Takht-i-Bahi are consisted of stupas, viharas, a central court, *uposathagara*s, *prāsāda*s, and other affiliated constructions such as yards, warehouses, corridors.

达赫德巴依佛寺遗址位于古代犍陀罗的中心，建筑遗迹主要分布在当地一座凸起山脉的北坡之上，东西绵延约 1.5 公里。但最重要的建筑遗迹位于遗址区的最东部，分布在三条南高北低的山脊中段，其中主体建筑位于最为宽阔的中间山脊之上。

1871 年，威尔彻主持了对该遗址中佛教遗迹部分的发掘；1875 年，康宁汉发表了其调查该遗址的详细报告；1907~1908 年，斯普纳对这处遗址进行了系统的考古发掘；1901~1911 年，哈格里夫斯再次对该遗址做了进一步清理。

遗址中的寺院遗迹主要包括主塔院、僧院、中庭、布萨处或讲堂，以及其他附属设施如院、仓、库、廊等。

The main entrance of the site seems to be laid on outside of the east wall. Walking along the valley from north to south through the entrance and then turning eastwards, the first spot we arrive, is the central court. Between the stupa court and vihara court is the lower central court with densely-located votive stupas in small sizes and varied styles. In the north, east and south around the central court, 29 independent Buddhist shrines are established with open side facing to the yard; Although the upper parts of the shrines are ruined, we can infer to certain confidence that they once had domes, like the shrines of the stupa court did. Among these shrines, those high narrow ones are most likely to have been the caves once with Buddha statue inside. A north-south brick-paved road stretched through the central court, connecting at one side the higher stupa court through 15 steps and at the other side the vihara court through 5 steps.

Climbing the 15 steps southwards from the central court, we arrive in the main stupa court. In its middle is a square pedestal with a few steps on its north side, which indicates that this is the spot of the main stupa. On the pedestal, a path used to be laid out for clockwise worship of the stupa. Around the main stupa, 5 open shrines had been designed to each of the three sides. At the very first, the 5 shrines were so constructed with a 0.86-meter distance between each other; then the interspaces were blocked off to form walls, on which small shrines were laid on for Buddha figures. In this way, these sacred shrines "sealed" the stupa court from three directions. If overviewing the whole architectural remains of Takht-i-Bahi, it comes out that upper buildings from ancient times are merely found in the stupa court: two and half shrines have their original roof retained. They are flat-cut domed roof supported by corbels; collars are found on the dome, and above the dome is another smaller inclined dome opening like a trefoil with a mushroom shaped steeple top.

据推测，寺院主入口在东院，由北向南沿沟而上，从入口到中庭东端，左转向西即可进入中庭之内。中庭位于主塔院与僧院之间，较两者地面低凹。里面还愿小塔密布，形制各异。其北、东、南三面建置佛龛，共 29 座，皆为独立式建筑，均面向中庭敞口；顶已塌毁，原为穹窿顶无疑，类似于主塔院中的那些佛龛，其中一些窄高的佛龛疑似为大像窟。一条南北向砖铺道路穿过中庭内分布的小塔及龛像，连通主塔院与僧院。两院的地面皆高于中庭，其中北侧的僧院通过一低矮五级踏道与中庭相连，而南侧的主塔院与中庭的踏道较高，有 15 级。

从中庭经过 15 级踏步向南进入主塔院。院中央为一方形台基，台基北面中央置踏步，正对塔院入口。此台基应是主塔塔基，主塔已残毁，塔基顶部原有右绕佛塔之礼拜道。塔院三面置佛龛，原来每面五座，每座佛龛皆向佛塔敞开。佛龛始建时，彼此间隔 0.86 米，后来为了增塑佛像，于每龛间补砌一横墙，形成类似佛龛的小神龛，故在东、南、西三面封闭了塔院。整个达赫德巴依遗址仅在主塔院保存有上层建筑，仅两座半佛龛保存了原始屋顶。佛龛之顶以托臂相承，呈穹顶，唯上部截平；穹顶之上另置系梁，上托另一小穹顶，外观呈斜顶形，平面半圆状；外立面敞口形如三叶，上为蘑菇形小尖顶。

5 steps northward from the central court is the vihara court, which is situated at a much lower spot than the stupa court, and is designated by scholars as the monastic quadrangle for the renounced Buddhist monks. The several parts of this court had made up the largest architectural group of the whole area and formed a compact unit of self-sufficiency. The vihara court has a square plan with altogether 15 buildings in south, west and north. A pool is laid on in the south-east, for which the roof drainage system of the buildings once had supplied water. In the middle of the east wall of the vihara court, a door leads to a 6.1-meter square kitchen, which once again has two doors on its north wall—the one connects another small room while the other is the exit to upstairs—and two side doors on its east wall—the real exits to outside, but to find two sustaining walls attached which seem to have served as bathrooms; going through the door of the south wall of the kitchen, one comes in a big room—apparently the dining hall. All roofs of these buildings do not exist anymore; however, they should have been a kind of overlaid dome structure.

In the north of this site, adjacent to the west of the vihara court, there is an open yard with high walls, and only one passage in the eastern part of the south wall. F.H. Wilcher suggested that it must have been the crematory whereas according to A. Cunningham, it was a gathering yard, while D.B. Spooner believed it as an assembly hall referring to the theory of A. Foucher. I am rather of the opinion that it was the spot of *uposathagara*, in which the Buddhist monks gathered on full-moon and new-moon days for religious praxis. The north and south walls of the *uposathagara* are based on the hills, and have almost retained their original erected height. Besides some lamp shrines in the inner walls of this yard, there are no windows and openings on the walls, and no traces of seats or other small structures on the ground. This square yard should have been initially designed for the *uposathagara*, a place for Buddhist monks for celebrating Buddhist rituals together. The high walls with only a

从中庭经过五级踏步向北进入僧院。僧院地面略低于塔院，此前学者大多称其为隐修院。这座僧院系一紧凑型的自给自足单元，是整个寺院群中体量最大的建筑。其平面呈方形，共有 15 座僧房置于南、西、北三面。僧院东南部存一水池，其水源来自僧房顶上的排水。僧院东墙中央，有门通向一 6.1 米见方的厨房。厨房北墙辟二门，一门通向另一小房，另一通往楼上；厨房东墙两端各辟一门，皆通往室外，室外有二凸起扶壁，似为厕所；南墙西侧有单门通往另一大房间——食堂。诸房舍屋顶皆不存，原为叠压式穹顶，但早已塌毁。

在遗址北部，紧靠僧院西侧，是一座较大的露天方院，围墙很高，仅南壁东侧开一门道。关于这座方院，威尔彻推测它应为荼毗之所，康宁汉认为是僧伽聚会之处，斯普纳根据富歇之说推想它原作会堂，笔者疑为汉译佛典之"布萨处"。布萨处的北墙和西墙自山坡起垒，迄今高耸。虽然这座方形建筑内壁有灯龛若干，但墙上既无窗洞，地面也未发现任何椅座或其他小型建筑遗迹。它应当是当初设计寺院时专门辟出的僧团集合修道场所——布萨处。单一门道与高墙，保证了隐蔽与静谧，除此之外很难想象它会充当别用。

犍陀罗的微笑 巴基斯坦古迹文物巡礼

single passage ensure serenity and secrecy. It is hard to imagine other proposing usage of this yard.

Further south from the *uposathagara* are the 10 rooms of the so-called "basement". Nevertheless, this architectural unit is rather built on a lower land than a constructive basement. The "basement" certainly came later into existence than the central court, for the way, it is attached to the west wall of the central court, shows that it did not belong to an earlier common constructive design. The roof of the basement is corbel arched, covered with thick mud, and has reached the parallel height of the ground of the central court. A. Cunningham presumed that these rooms of the basement were used as the warehouses of Takht-i-Bahi.

Further south from the "basements" is another square court with a stairway leading to the valley. On the pedestal of its south wall, there are 6 clay molded footprints of standing Buddhas. Several huge clay-molded Buddha heads had been unearthed from this site, hence making it known as "the Court of Monumental Buddhas".

The architectural remains of Takht-i-Bahi serve as a model typical for the Gandhara Buddhist monastery, of which the stupa and vihara courts formed the most crucial parts.

Li Xiao, Duan Qing

布萨处南侧，是十间所谓"地下室"。但实际上它们并不是真正的地下室，只是建在低洼处而已。其年代较中庭为晚，因其倚中庭西墙而建，绝非砌合而成；顶为突拱结构，上覆厚泥，与中庭地面齐平。康宁汉推测：这些房舍应为整个寺院之库藏。

在"地下室"之南，有另一方院及其下面通往山谷的梯道。其中，方院南墙下部的基坛上残存六身泥塑大立佛足迹，院中出土泥塑大佛头若干，故俗称"大像院"。

达赫德巴依遗址中的寺院遗迹，堪称犍陀罗僧伽蓝或寺院的典范。其中塔院和僧院是最重要的组成部分。

李肖

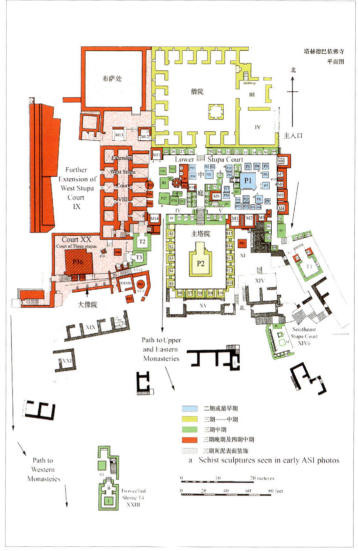

达赫德巴依遗址航拍图

摄影 任超

Aerial View of Takht-i-Bahi Complex

Photographed by Ren Chao

达赫德巴依佛寺平面图

Plan of Takht-i-Bahi sacred area

主塔院复原效果图

The Plan of the main stupa court

达赫德巴依遗址航拍全景

摄影 任超

Aerial View of Takht-i-Bahi Complex

Photographed by Ren Chao

主塔塔基

摄影 孟嗣徽

Pedestal of the main stupa

Photographed by Meng Sihui

主塔院上层建筑残存的佛龛

摄影 李肖

The remained Buddhist shrines in upper structures
in southern stupa court

Photographed by Li Xiao

主塔院佛龛之顶的托臂结构

摄影 李肖

Corbel structure at the top of a Buddhist shrine

Photographed by Li Xiao

主塔院完整之佛龛

摄影 梁鉴

An almost intact Buddhist shrine

Photographed by Liang Jian

达赫德巴依航拍俯视图

摄影 任超

Aerial view of the Takht-i-Bahi complex

Photographed by Ren Chao

PESHAWAR MUSEUM

白沙瓦博物馆

Since ancient time, the Gandhara region has been distinctive for its position as a transit zone. If sailing through time back to centuries before and after the Common Era, we might meet such names as for instance Gandhara in the Old Persian inscriptions when the region was a satrapy or province of the Achaemenid empire. The army of Alexander the Great advanced along the Kabul river and was obliged to give up pushing further at the door of the first rising Indian empire, that of the Mauryas (324-187 B.C.). It was generally ascribed to Ashoka, the greatest emperor of Mauryas, that Buddhism began to flourish. The Dharmarajika Stupa in Taxila is supposed to be dated back to his era. The Maurya dynasty was replaced in the second half of the 2nd century B.C. by the Shuṅga rulers while the Graeco-Bactrians moved in, established themselves in Gandhara and other adjacent regions and have led to their being called "Indo-Greeks." Perhaps at the same time the *Sakas* came whose migrations along routes through northern Pakistan, Afghanistan, and Iran profoundly affected South Asian political and cultural history during at least the 1st century B.C. and 1st century A.D..As proven by inscriptions and coins, *Sakas* have left their impact on ancient Indian history for a period of about 500 years (c. 1st century B.C. through 4th century A.D.).

It would certainly be a difficult task to try to describe the rise of the Kushans in a few sentences. The successful expansion of Kushanes in the 1st century A.D. is traceable through Chinese historical records and numismatic and epigraphic sources in South Asia. The 2nd century saw the Kushans establish a great empire and hold sway between the powers of the Romans in the West and of the Chinese in the East.

当我们的车驶入白沙瓦博物馆的院落，迎接我们的是凝重的红色和点缀其中的浓郁的绿色。或许那天刚好在下雨，一幢红砂岩的建筑映入眼帘。房前种植了热带的绿植，虽然不多，却装点出院落的宁静，衬托出洁净。白沙瓦博物馆建造于 1907 年，其建筑风格据说融合了英式、传统印度式以及伊斯兰的建筑风格。伊斯兰的风格容易辨认：搭建在房屋顶上的凉亭，凉亭上八角基座上的圆顶，那是伊斯兰的特征。建在屋顶的露台，或许体现了英式。而所谓印度式，大约就是红砂岩的颜色而令人想起印度的神庙吧。

They were acting as the effective intermediaries over the Eurasian overland and could extend their political, economic and cultural influence from Bactria and northern India even to areas of eastern Central Asia in the southern Tarim Basin, while absorbing cultural elements from Greek, Roman and Chinese. Hidden behind the huge quantity of surviving sculptures and large number of sites spread over the Gandhara region is the background of the generous patronage of the huge empire of Kushans, well known for its possession of a commercial importance and consequent wealth. The Dynasty of Kushans expired eventually, but this fact did not hinder the Gandhara region in following centuries to receive further migration waves of *Kidārites*, *Hephthalites*, just to name a few moments in the history of the Gandhara region. The manifold styles and patterns shown in sculptures and religious artifacts would have been the result of pluralism of population that came and settled down in the Gandhara region which inevitably left their cultural and imaginary imprints on various subjects. Thus, a short notice of migration of diverse peoples into Gandhara region is necessary before going to observe the remains of Gandhara Buddhist art. Peoples like Graeco-Bactrians, *Sakas* and even Kushans, had certainly held their own religions before becoming patronage of Buddhism. Their productivities and artistic imaginaries have for sure contributed to the richness of Gandhara Buddhist art.

Duan Qing

白沙瓦博物馆主要收藏佛教造像。白沙瓦历史上曾是贵霜王朝的文化中心。贵霜王朝庇护佛教，白沙瓦周边尽是佛教的遗址。自 19 世纪末 20 世纪初，英法对犍陀罗地区佛教遗址的发掘，使大量的佛教艺术造像重现天日。这些艺术品，例如马尔丹地区 11 处遗址出土的艺术品，大部分收藏在白沙瓦博物馆，形成了白沙瓦博物馆最鲜明的特色，使其在世界上独享盛名。

走进白沙瓦博物馆，仿佛穿越了时空，回到一千几百年前的犍陀罗，站在曾经浸润了这片土地的佛教艺术的空间中。正中间的展厅展出几尊佛的立像。这些佛像发式不同，衣着类似。它们原本属于寺院，属于宗教氛围的神圣的空间，作为宗教仪式、寺院生活的不可缺少的一部分。世事变迁，曾经繁荣的寺院早已成断壁残垣，成为废墟。佛像也失去了充当仪式主角的功能。最终，是白沙瓦博物馆成为这些佛像的庇护所，可以令人在和平安宁中欣赏这些几乎是二千年前的艺术创作。

段晴

STANDING BUDDHAS

佛立像

Peshawar museum is sheltering numerous standing Buddhas of stone-work. Two general remarks are noteworthy: Firstly, all of these sculptures made of stone are remarkably not free-standing statues, which means that they must originally stand in tall niches with backs against walls so that carving at the backside of statues is not necessary. Secondly, it is easy to see behind each Buddha statue the great endeavor of ancient artisans for attempting to transform the animated charm of Shakyamuni onto the lifeless stone. As related in *Lalitavistara*, a crucial Buddhist text of the *Sarvastivadins*, after Shakyamuni had retained the Enlightenment, he decided to give his first teachings to the five former companions when he was practicing austerities. When Shakyamuni was nearing them, the five were deeply impressed by his brightness which was radiating from his face and sense organs that they instantly received from him the teaching in Buddhist dharma, the ordination and became the first monks of a Buddhist samgha. *Lalitavistara* is a scripture of the school of the *Sarvastivadins* which must be popular during the 2nd and 3rd centuries in Gandhara region. The scene of Shakyamuni to come to his first followers and the establishment of the 3 jewels (Buddha, dharma and samgha) as described in *Lalitavistara* could have impacted artisans' work. It might also have been a request from donators for the ancient artisans that they should try their best to transform the majestic and amiable appearance of Buddha into lifeless stone, and the success of ancient artisans' work is preserved till today.

白沙瓦博物馆的佛立像十分惹人瞩目。站在这些石头的雕像面前，两层思路浮现脑海。仔细观察，可发现这些石雕造像并非囫囵完整，正面以及双侧雕塑完整，而后背并未雕塑。由此可知，这些造像原是摆放在量身定制的神龛里，背部靠墙，所以无需雕琢。这些立像，造型优美，尤其是面部看上去竟然十分生动。可以想见，近两千年前的石匠必然曾经倾注了大量精力，才令石头上生出生动的感觉。汉译佛经有公元 308 年前后译出的《普曜经》，又有 7 世纪后半叶译出的《方广大庄严经》。一般认为，这是说一切有部的文献之一。犍陀罗地区，在贵霜时代，多有寺院属于说一切有部。上述作品的现存梵语版本第 26 章，讲述释迦牟尼放弃了苦修之后，终于在菩提树下悟道成佛。他决定首先向自己苦修的伙伴宣说佛法。当他来到鹿野苑，那五人惊异于释迦牟尼非凡的面相，他们对佛说："长老瞿昙！面目端正诸根寂静，身相光明如阎浮金及詹波花，瞿昙！今者应证出世圣种智耶？"后来佛为他们说法，这五人成为佛教僧团的第一批僧侣。这就是佛教三宝，即"佛"、"法"、"僧"的诞生过程。而在此过程中，成佛的释迦牟尼面目端正，周身散发的非凡魅力起到了关键性的作用。可以想象，在说一切有部流行的地域，将佛非凡的魅力表现在石雕造像上，应是对石匠的要求，也是石匠努力实现的目标。应该说，公元 2~3 世纪的石匠将佛的魅力完美地融入了石雕造像之中。

Because of a short stay, it was impossible for us to measure the height of every statue. General impression: they are a little bit taller than an average man's height. Besides, the collection of standing Buddha statues is quite numerous. They were either excavated from a Buddhist site, or purchased in last century. In this section, only specimen with an exact archaeological provenance are selected which are already sufficient to offer a glimpse into the varieties of Buddhist art in ancient world.

Duan Qing

这里需要提前说明的是，由于停留时间短暂，我们未能实地测量这些立像的尺寸。基本印象：略高于真人的身高吧。白沙瓦博物馆可以看到的佛立像为数不少，有些来自佛教遗址，有些则是买入或者捐赠。本节仅选择有明确出土地点者。但这些佛像已足以令我们见识古代犍陀罗地区多姿多彩的佛教艺术。

段晴

佛立像，公元 2~3 世纪
萨合力巴洛尔 1909~1910 发掘，片岩

摄影 任超

Standing Buddha, 2nd-3rd century A.D.,
excavated from Sahri Bahlol during 1909-1910, grey schist

Photographed by Ren Chao

佛立像，公元 2~3 世纪，藏品 2854，
萨合力巴洛尔 1909~1910，片岩

摄影 任超

Standing Buddha, 2nd-3rd century,
excavated from Sahri Bahlol during 1909-1910. No. 2854, grey schist.

Photographed by Ren Chao

佛立像，公元 2~3 世纪，
萨合力巴洛尔 1909~1910，片岩

摄影 任超

Standing Buddha, 2nd-3rd century,
excavated from Sahri Bahlol during 1909-1910, grey schist.

Photographed by Ren Chao

佛立像，公元 2~3 世纪，
达赫德巴依 1906-1907 年发掘，片岩

摄影 任超

Standing Buddha, 2nd-3rd century,
excavated from Takhti-i-Bahi during 1906-1907, grey schist.

Photographed by Ren Chao

犍陀罗的微笑

巴基斯坦古迹文物巡礼

佛立像，公元 2~3 世纪，
达赫德巴依 1913 年发掘，片岩

摄影 任超

Standing Buddha, 2nd-3rd century,
excavated from Takhti-i-Bahi during 1913, grey schist.

Photographed by Ren Chao

佛立像，公元 2~3 世纪，
达赫德巴依 1912 年发掘，片岩

摄影 任超

Standing Buddha, 2nd-3rd century,
excavated from Takhti-i-Bahi during 1912, grey schist.

Photographed by Ren Chao

佛立像，公元 2~3 世纪
达赫德巴依 1913 年发掘，片岩

摄影 任超

Standing Buddha, 2nd-3rd century,
excavated from Takhti-i-Bahi during 1913, grey schist.

Photographed by Ren Chao

SEATED BUDDHAS

佛坐像

Dhyāna or Buddhist meditation is one of the most important means for attaining Enlightenment. So it is respectfully to find images of seated Buddha in Buddhist sites and museums over the Gandhara region. Peshawar museum shelters quite a few independent seated Buddha statues which, like the standing statues uncarved at the backside, may have also served as cult images in ancient monasteries. To our regret, no detailed accounts about their original origin could be noticed during a very short visit to the museum. Several labels beside the statues inform that they are either purchased or granted in early decades of last century to the museum. As far as the size of the statues shown below is concerned, Ren Chao, our photographer told from his impression that the seated images of Buddha have a height of 70-80 cm.

The seated images of the Buddha are quite standardized. Apart from common attributes of Buddha, a seated Buddha statue is usually depicted in cross-legged meditation posture. Varieties are shown indeed in detail. In this section, three of the seated Buddha statues are picked out from the collection of Peshawar Museum, in order to demonstrate some varied details.

Duan Qing

至少在佛教发展初期，戒、定、慧是佛教实现最高理想的必经途径。当年释迦牟尼在菩提树下通过修习禅定而悟道，悟道之后而说法。因此，刻画禅定中的佛理所当然成为佛最典型的表现形式。白沙瓦博物馆收藏有多尊佛独立的坐像，一如佛的立像，曾经位于神圣的殿堂，背面抵墙，接受各种仪式各种崇拜，所以佛像的背部基本未经过雕琢。我们在白沙瓦博物馆停留的时间毕竟太过短暂，未能详尽了解这些佛坐像的出土地点。一些标签显示，多数是博物馆在上世纪最初几十年内获得的捐赠品，或者是购入的。依据摄影师任超的目测，这些坐像的高度大约在 70~80 厘米之间。

坐像表现似乎是一致的，呈跏趺坐，这是禅定的基本坐姿。但是细观察，独立的坐像与坐像之间还是有诸多细节方面的表现不一。

段晴

禅定佛坐像

摄影 任超

Buddha in meditation

Photographed by Ren Chao

犍陀罗的微笑

巴基斯坦古迹文物巡礼

禅定佛坐像，公元 2~3 世纪，
白沙瓦博物馆，片岩

摄影 任超

Meditating Buddha, 2nd-3rd century,
Peshawar Museum, grey schist

Photographed by Ren Chao

禅定佛坐像基座浮雕

摄 影 任 超

Meditating Buddha, relief on the pedestal.

Photographed by Ren Chao

佛坐像，公元 2~3 世纪，
白沙瓦博物馆，片岩

摄影 任超

Seated Buddha, 2nd-3rd century,
Peshawar Museum, grey schist

Photographed by Ren Chao

佛坐像 基座浮雕

摄影 任超

Seated Buddha, relief on the pedestal.

Photographed by Ren Chao

BODHISATTVAS

菩萨像

In preparing this volume, by choosing and selecting photos and pictures of Gandhara Buddhist art, we made during the journey in April 2018, principle was decided that concerns about big problems such as whether or not the Gandhara art was a product of Mahāyāna Buddhism should not be touched. Now going to the sculptures of Bodhisattvas, the question about Hinayāna or Mahāyāna compellingly comes into my mind. Generally speaking, the appearance of bodhisattvas is regarded as one of the clearest phenomena for indicating the prevalence of Mahāyāna Buddhism. After checking the sculptures so far we have seen, however, the number of bodhisattva images is not persuasive enough for alleging that the Gandhara art of Buddhism is representative for Mahāyāna Buddhism. For instance, the popular 8 great Bodhisattvas as we usually encounter in Mahāyāna texts are missing for their artistic presentation. At this stage it is preferable to leave the problem as it is by citing from an expertise statement: "Foucher, while denying any Mahāyāna character to Gandhāra art, cautiously believed that Mahāyāna concerns emerged towards the end of the school and might be expressed by an older iconography, but a contrary view has held that the Buddha image, present almost from the beginning of Gandhāra sculpture, owes its origin to Mahāyāna developments and that this must bear on the sectarian affiliation of the art." (W. Zwalf, *A Catalogue of the Gandhāra Sculpture*, volume I, Text, published for the Trustees of the British Museum by British Museum Press, 1996, 32.)

Duan Qing

关于菩萨像，一些疑问还是挥之不去，例如，犍陀罗的佛教艺术作品是否属于大乘，抑或不是？众所周知，菩萨出现是佛教进入大乘的重要标识之一。这恰是疑问所在。在白沙瓦博物馆浏览那些造像时，我曾留意找寻所熟悉的八大菩萨的身影，然而并未找到。在此似乎不宜纠结于这么庞大的问题，以前辈学者的见解作为这一节开篇的叙述，似更相宜：

"富歇一方面认为犍陀罗艺术中没有大乘的特征，却也小心翼翼地提出，大乘的主张已经出现于部派晚期，或许是以古老的造像表现出来。但是，相反的观点认为，佛的造像几乎出现在犍陀罗造像滥觞时期，其起源应追溯到大乘的发展，并且影响到部派佛教的艺术。"

段晴

左图：弥勒菩萨立像，公元2~3 世纪，萨合力巴洛尔 1912 年发掘
上图：基座浮雕

摄影　任超

Standing Maitreya (left), statue on the pedestal, 2nd-3rd century,
excavated from the site Sahri Bahlol in1912, grey schist.

Relief on the pedestal (above)

Photographed by Ren Chao

弥勒菩萨像，公元2~3 世纪，萨合力巴洛尔 1912 年发掘，片岩

摄影 任超

Maitreya, 2nd-3rd century,
excavated from Sahri Bahlol in1912, grey schist.

Photographed by Ren Chao

菩萨立像，公元 2~3 世纪，达赫德巴依 1907~1908 年发掘，片岩

摄影 任超

Standing Buddisattva, 2nd-3rd century,
excavated from Takht-i-Bahi during 1907-1908, grey schist.

Photographed by Ren Chao

THE PROPHECY OF DĪPAṂKARA AND BUDDHA'S LIFE STORIES

"燃灯佛授记"与佛传故事

One of the main focuses of the Gandhara Buddhist art was the Buddha's life story, including many episodes from his birth to death and his miracles. Almost all the important life scenes of the historic Buddha were beautifully and liberally represented in the Gandharan art. Just to name a few, Siddhartha's birth under the tree, school scene, marriage scene, first meditation, the great departure, six years' fasting, enlightenment under the Bodhi tree, the first sermon, the miracle at Srāvasti, nirvāna scene, distribution of the relics, etc.

犍陀罗佛教艺术的核心主题之一是佛传故事，包括从降生到涅槃的众多情节，以及佛陀的神变。佛的生平的几乎所有重要场景，都在犍陀罗艺术中得到了精美、自由的表现。例如，树下降生、入学、纳妃、初禅、逾城出家、六年苦行、树下悟道、初转法轮、舍卫城神变、涅槃、分舍利等等。

An important cultural heritage of the Gandharan Buddhist sites is a series of reliefs carved with Buddha's life stories, which are sequentially arranged around the podium or the railings of the stupas. Among them, the prophecy of "Dīpaṃkara" has always been the beginning of the narrative cycle. The representations of this prophecy are rarely seen in Central India and other regions where Buddhism had been dominant, but are amazingly numerous in Gandhara area and are always seen in the Gandharan sculpture collections of museums worldwide. This makes the motif crucial. In all of the Buddha's past life practices, the prophecy of "Dīpaṃkara" is a key point. As is one of the past Buddhas, Dīpaṃkara had made the prophecy that Shakyamuni would be the Buddha in the future. It is the end of the series of Jātakas, as well as the beginning of the life story of Shakyamuni Buddha. Buddhists believe that there had been a succession of many Buddhas in the distant past and that many more will appear in the future. Since then, prophecy (vyākaraṇa) has been a traditional way to confirm who will be the Buddha in the next circle of life. For example, Shakyamuni predicts that Maitreya will be the next Buddha in the future.

The idea of vyākaraṇa has been imported to China since Buddhism was first introduced. "The Prophecy of Dīpaṃkara" could be widely seen in Chinese Buddhist Sutras, such as Cāryanidāna of the Eastern Han Dynasty, Sūtra on the Life of the Prince in accordance with Good Omens of the Eastern Wu Dynasty, Lalitavistara and Sūtra on Past and Present Causes and Effects of the Western Jin Dynasty, Sūtra on Past and Present Causes and Effects of the Song period of the Southern Dynasties, and Abhiniṣkramaṇa-Sūtra of the Sui Dynasty. Among the composers and translators of these sutras, Aśvaghoṣa was a mentor and friend of Kaniska, the emperor of the Kushan Empire while Zhi Qian of the Eastern Wu Dynasty and Dharmarakṣa of the Western Jin Dynasty were from Yuezhi, Abhiniṣkramaṇa Sūtra was compiled in Uddyāna, on the north of Gandhara, and the translator Jñānagupta was also from Gandhara.

以佛传（佛本行）内容为题材并连续排列在塔基或围栏上的石刻浮雕，是犍陀罗佛教留存下来的主要遗迹。在这些佛传故事雕刻中，通常以"燃灯佛授记"作为佛传故事的开篇。这在中印度乃至其他佛教地区是十分罕见的内容，在犍陀罗本土和世界各地博物馆中所遗存的犍陀罗佛传雕刻中，"燃灯佛授记"的数量之多令人称奇，使这一题材显得格外重要。在释迦牟尼的历劫修行中，"燃灯佛授记"是其成就佛陀的关键：作为过去佛的燃灯佛预言释迦牟尼将在未来成佛。从逻辑上讲，燃灯佛授记既是讲述释迦牟尼历劫修行本生故事的终结，又是释迦牟尼修行成道佛传故事的开端，其意义重大。其后，这种通过"授记"传法的方式被延续下来，如释迦牟尼授记弥勒菩萨将在未来成佛与此是一脉相承的。

在中国，这种"授记"思想在佛教传入之初就进入中国了。"燃灯佛为释迦牟尼授记"的内容广泛出现在汉文经典中，如东汉《修行本起经》，东吴《太子瑞应本起经》，西晋《普曜经》和《过去现在因果经》，南朝宋《过去现在因果经》，隋《佛本行集经》等。其中编撰与译经者：东吴的支谦和西晋的竺法护都是月氏人；马鸣菩萨则是贵霜国王迦腻色伽的良师益友。集佛本行故事之大成的《佛本行集经》，产生于犍陀罗国北方的乌仗那国，译者阇那崛多是犍陀罗人。

犍陀罗的微笑

巴基斯坦古迹文物巡礼

The scene of "the Prophecy of Dīpaṃkara" is carved in accordance with the story in the sutras. The story happened outside of a city gate. Plot 1: a young boy (the former life of Shakyamuni) is buying lotuses from Gopika. Gopika is holding a vase and lotuses. The young boy is wearing a buckskin skirt, holding a purse to make the deal. Plot 2: the young boy is throwing the lotuses above Dīpaṃkara. The lotuses stays there. Plot 3: Dīpaṃkara raises his right hand, giving the prophecy to the young boy. Plot 4: the young boy is putting his palms together, kneeling, and suddenly flying into the sky. Plot 5: after coming back to the earth, the young boy is kneeling down and worshiping Dīpaṃkara, putting his hair on the wet soil for Dīpaṃkara to walk on. Most of the Gandharan reliefs in Peshawar and Swat depicted these five plots. Comparing with the reliefs of Buddha's life stories in Central India, the Gandharan sculptures have a much clearer structure of representing the story – any figures, animals and other botanic background, which have nothing to do with the scenario have all been left out.

Generally speaking, in the earliest stage of the development of Buddhist art, the image of the Buddha in human form had not been noticed. It is widely accepted that Gandhara and Mathura are the two centers where the images of the Buddha in human form were first sculpted between the 1st century B.C. and the 1st century A.D., under the reign of the Kushan empire. The open-minded Kushans adopted many different beliefs and customs, including Buddhism and elements of the Hellenistic culture of Bactria. Therefore we can see diverse mythological values and associated legends in various figural depictions, which have achieved an aesthetic harmony in the entire composition. As some scholars have observed, the future Buddha Maitreya may sometimes have been statued next to the Buddha Shakyamuni. And there are also other Bodhisattva images which are not found in the earlier school of Buddhist art.

围绕着经文而展开的犍陀罗雕刻"燃灯佛授记"恰如其分地表现出这些情节：故事场景发生在一座城的城门外。情节一：儒童（释迦牟尼的前世）向瞿夷买花，瞿夷手执水瓶和莲花，儒童腰围鹿皮衣，手执钱袋与之交易；情节二：儒童将青莲花抛向燃灯佛的上方，莲花在佛陀上方停立；情节三：燃灯佛扬右掌为儒童授记；情节四：儒童双手合十作跪踞状陡然升空；情节五：儒童落地后稽首佛足为佛布发掩泥。白沙瓦和斯瓦特地区的犍陀罗雕刻"燃灯佛授记"，大约都选择了这五个情节。可以看出，与中印度的"佛传"雕刻相比，犍陀罗雕刻的叙事结构简单明了，与故事情节没有关系的人物、动物以及植物等背景雕刻均被省略到极致。

大体说来，在佛教艺术发展的最初阶段，拟人化的佛像尚未出现。一般认为犍陀罗与秣菟罗是公元前后拟人化佛像起源的两个中心，都是在贵霜王朝治下。贵霜人思想开放，吸纳了多种不同的信仰与习俗，包括佛教与大夏的希腊化元素。因此，我们可以在各种象征化的表现中，看到不同的神话价值观与相关传说，在整个构图中达成美学上的和谐。正如有学者所观察到的，未来佛弥勒有时会与释迦牟尼佛相邻。此外，还有一些菩萨像，在早先的佛教艺术流派中从未出现过。

The sculptors of this area, taking advantage of contacts with the Greeks, Romans, Persians and Central Asians, making use of their motifs and technology, translated the Buddhist biographical texts into vivid details in stone, stucco, terracotta, bronze, and even paintings; and thus facilitated the expansion of Buddhism along the Silk Roads through the travels of pilgrims and traders. Most of the stories are displayed in the stupas and monasteries all over the entire Gandharan region, especially carved onto the podium or the railings of the stupas. The reliefs with Buddha's life scenes generally measure 20 to 40 cm in width and 10 to 30 cm in height, although some large ones can be more than 60 cm in width and height. The renowned Chinese pilgrim Xuan Zang went to Gandhara in ca. 629 A.D., who recorded a lot of such stupas.

The Gandhara Buddhist art flourished during the Kushan period. Unfortunately, the decline of the art started in the 5th century. Some scholars blame the devastation of the White Huns for the end of this glorious art, while others hold Sassanian invasions, the introduction of stucco images in the 3rd-4th centuries, as well as a revival of Hindu elements responsible.

Meng Sihui, Chen Hao, Fan Jingjing

这一地区的工匠利用与希腊人、罗马人、波斯人、中亚人交往的有利条件，借用他们的母题与技术，将佛典中的佛传故事生动具体地刻画到石头、灰泥、陶土、青铜甚至壁画上，经由朝圣者与商人的旅行，促进了佛教在丝绸之路沿线的传播。在整个犍陀罗地区，大多数佛传故事被艺术化地表现于佛塔上或佛寺中，尤其是被雕刻在佛塔的塔基或围栏上。大体而言，佛传故事浮雕宽 20 至 40 厘米，高 10 到 30 厘米，但也有一些大浮雕的长、宽都超过了 60 厘米。汉地求法高僧玄奘约在 629 年到达犍陀罗地区，在《大唐西域记》中记载了不少这样的佛塔。

犍陀罗佛教艺术在贵霜时期发展昌盛，却在 5 世纪左右开始衰败。一些学者归因于白匈奴的破坏活动。另一些学者则认为还有萨珊入侵、3 至 4 世纪时灰泥塑像的出现、印度教元素的复兴等多重因素。

孟嗣徽，范晶晶

犍陀罗的微笑

巴基斯坦古迹文物巡礼

燃灯佛授记，2~3 世纪，片岩，
白沙瓦博物馆，藏品号 2718

摄影 孟嗣徽

Dīpaṃkara Jātaka, 2nd-3rd century, schist,
Peshawar Museum, No.2718.

Photographed by Meng Sihui

　　THE PROPHECY OF DĪPAṂKARA AND BUDDHA'S LIFE STORIES　/　"燃灯佛授记"与佛传故事

燃灯佛授记，2~3 世纪，达赫德巴依 1907~1908 年发掘，片岩，
白沙瓦博物馆，藏品号 2720

摄影 孟嗣徽

Dīpaṃkara Jātaka, 2nd-3rd century, Takht-i-bahi, exc.1907-1908, schist,
Peshawar Museum, No.2720.

Photographed by Meng Sihui

燃灯佛授记（上部），2~3 世纪，萨合力巴洛尔 1908~1910 年发掘，片岩，
白沙瓦博物馆，藏品号 2810

摄影 孟嗣徽

*Dīpaṃkara Jātaka (the top), 2nd-3rd century, Sahri Bahlol , exc.1908-1910, schist,
Peshawar Museum, No.2810.*

Photographed by Meng Sihui

燃灯佛授记，2~3 世纪，萨合力巴洛尔 1909~1910 年发掘，片岩，
白沙瓦博物馆，藏品号 2721

摄影 孟嗣徽

*Dīpaṃkara Jātaka, 2nd-3rd century, Sahri Bahlol, exc.1909-1910, schist,
Peshawar Museum, No.2721.*

Photographed by Meng Sihui

燃灯佛授记，2~3 世纪，萨合力巴洛尔 1906~1907 年发掘，片岩，
白沙瓦博物馆，藏品号 2719

摄影 孟嗣徽

Dīpaṃkara Jātaka, 2nd-3rd century, Sahri Bahlol, exc.1906-1907, schist,
Peshawar Museum, No.2719.

Photographed by Meng Sihui

燃灯佛授记，2 世纪，希克里 1888 年发掘，片岩，
拉合尔博物馆

摄影 梁鉴

Dīpaṃkara Jātaka, 2nd century, Sikri, exc.1888,
schist, Lahore Museum.

Photographed by Liang Jian

燃灯佛授记，2 世纪，希克里 1889 年发掘，片岩，
拉合尔博物馆

摄影 梁鉴

Dīpaṃkara Jātaka, 2nd century, Sikri, exc.1889,
schist, Lahore Museum.

Photographed by Liang Jian

GANDHARA'S SMILE
THE TOUR OF CULTURAL RELICS IN PAKISTAN

白象入胎，2~3 世纪，萨合力巴洛尔 1906~1907 年发掘，片岩
白沙瓦博物馆，藏品号 2722

摄影 任超

Dream scene, 2nd-3rd century, Sahri Bahlol, exc. 1906-1907, schist
Peshawar Museum, No. 2722.

Photographed by Ren Chao

白象入胎，2~3 世纪，萨合力巴洛尔，捐赠，片岩，白沙瓦博物馆，藏品号 2723

摄影 任超

Dream scene, 2nd-3rd century, Sahri Bahlol, donation, schist, Peshawar Museum, No. 2723.

Photographed by Ren Chao

树下降生，2~3 世纪，巴利科特，捐赠，白沙瓦博物馆，藏品号 2727

摄影 任超

Birth scene, 2nd-3rd century, Barikot, Peshawar Museum, No. 2727.

Photographed by Ren Chao

相师占梦，2~3 世纪，马尔丹收集，白沙瓦博物馆，藏品号 2724

摄 影 任 超

Interpretation of the dream, 2nd-3rd century, received from Mardan Guides Mess, Peshawar Museum, No. 2724.

Photographed by Ren Chao

GANDHARA'S SMILE
THE TOUR OF CULTURAL RELICS IN PAKISTAN

No. 2725

树下降生，2~3 世纪，萨合力巴洛尔 1906-1907 年发掘，片岩
白沙瓦博物馆，藏品号 2725

摄影 任超

Birth scene, 2nd-3rd century, Sahri Bahlol, exc. 1906-1907, schist,
Peshawar Museum, No. 2725.

Photographed by Ren Chao

树下降生，2~3 世纪，白沙瓦博物馆，藏品号 2729

摄影 任超

Birth scene, 2nd-3rd century, Peshawar Museum, No. 2729.

Photographed by Ren Chao

浴佛，2~3 世纪，马尔丹收集，
白沙瓦博物馆，藏品号 2728

摄影 任超

Bath scene, 2nd-3rd century, received from Mardan Guides Mess,
Peshawar Museum, No. 2728.

Photographed by Ren Chao

浴佛，2~3 世纪，
白沙瓦博物馆，藏品号 2733

摄影 任超

Bath scene, 2nd-3rd century,
Peshawar Museum, No. 2733.

Photographed by Ren Chao

堕地行七步，公元 2~3 世纪，马尔丹收集，
白沙瓦博物馆，藏品号 2731

摄影 任超

The first seven steps, 2nd-3rd century, received from Mardan Guides Mess, Peshawar Museum, No. 2731.

Photographed by Ren Chao

仙人预言，2~3 世纪，萨合力巴洛尔 1906~1907 年发掘，
白沙瓦博物馆，藏品号 2734

摄影 任超

Horoscope scene, 2nd-3rd century, Sahri Bahlol, exc. 1906-1907, Peshawar Museum, No. 2734.

Photographed by Ren Chao

犍陀罗的微笑

巴基斯坦古迹文物巡礼

GANDHARA'S SMILE
THE TOUR OF CULTURAL RELICS IN PAKISTAN

太子上学，2~3 世纪，萨合力巴洛尔
1911~1912 年发掘，片岩
白沙瓦博物馆，藏品号 2736

摄影 任超

School scene, 2nd-3rd century, Sahri Bahlol,
exc. 1911-1912, schist,
Peshawar Museum, No. 2736.

Photographed by Ren Chao

太子上学，2~3 世纪，捐赠，
白沙瓦博物馆，藏品号 2737

摄影 任超

School scene, 2nd-3rd century,
Peshawar Museum, No. 2737.

Photographed by Ren Chao

树下初禅，2~3 世纪，萨合力巴洛尔
1911~1912 年发掘，片岩
白沙瓦博物馆，藏品号 2750

摄影 任超

First meditation, 2nd-3rd century, Sahri Bahlol,
exc. 1911-1912, schist,
Peshawar Museum, No. 2750.

Photographed by Ren Chao

犍陀罗的微笑

巴基斯坦古迹文物巡礼

纳妃，2~3 世纪，捐赠，
白沙瓦博物馆，藏品号 2747

摄影 范晶晶

Marriage scene, 2nd-3rd century,
Peshawar Museum, No. 2747

Photographed by Fan Jingjing

纳妃，2~3 世纪，
白沙瓦博物馆，藏品号 2748

摄影 范晶晶

Marriage scene, 2nd-3rd century,
Peshawar Museum, No. 2748.

Photographed by Fan Jingjing

宫廷场景与出城见病人，2~3 世纪，1950 年购于拉赫尔斯瓦比，
白沙瓦博物馆，藏品号 2751

摄 影 任 超

Palace and street scenes, 2nd-3rd century, purchased at Lahore Swabi in 1950, Peshawar Museum,
No. 2751.

Photographed by Ren Chao

宫廷场景与逾城出家，2~3 世纪，1903 年由印度考古局长收购，
白沙瓦博物馆，藏品号 2754

摄影 范晶晶

Palace scene and the great departure, 2nd- 3rd century, purchased by D.G.A. Survey of India in 1903,
Peshawar Museum, No. 2754

Photographed by Fan Jingjing

THE PROPHECY OF DĪPAṂKARA AND BUDDHA'S LIFE STORIES / "燃灯佛授记"与佛传故事

逾城出家，2~3 世纪，1934 年收购，
白沙瓦博物馆，藏品号 2752

摄影　任超

The great departure, 2nd-3rd century, purchased in 1934, Peshawar Museum, No. 2752.

Photographed by Ren Chao

逾城出家，2~3 世纪，萨合力巴洛尔，1911~1912 年发掘，片岩
白沙瓦博物馆，藏品号 2753

摄影　任超

The great departure, 2nd-3rd century, Sahri Bahlol, exc. 1911-1912, schist, Peshawar Museum, No. 2753

Photographed by Ren Chao

妇女昏睡，2~3 世纪，法王塔发掘，千枚岩，
塔克西拉博物馆

摄影 任超

Sleep of the women, 2nd-3rd century, Dharmarajika exc., phyllite,
Taxila Museum.

Photographed by Ren Chao

妇女昏睡，2~3 世纪，法王塔发掘，千枚岩，
塔克西拉博物馆

摄影 任超

Sleep of the women, 2nd-3rd century, Dharmarajika exc., phyllite,
Taxila Museum.

Photographed by Ren Chao

犍陟告别，2~3 世纪，捐赠，
白沙瓦博物馆，藏品号 2755

摄影 范晶晶

Farewell of Kanthaka, 2nd-3rd century, donation,
Peshawar Museum, No. 2755.

Photographed by Fan Jingjing

GANDHARA'S SMILE
THE TOUR OF CULTURAL RELICS IN PAKISTAN

拜佛头巾，2~3 世纪，马尔丹收集，
白沙瓦博物馆，藏品号 2846

摄影 任超

Worship of the turban, 2nd-3rd century,
received from Mardan Guides Mess,
Peshawar Museum, No. 2846.

Photographed by Ren Chao

悉达多苦修像，公元 2~3 世纪，达赫德巴依
1907~1908 年发掘，片岩

摄影 任超

Fasting Siddhārtha, 2nd-3rd century, excavated from
Takhti-i-Bahi during 1907-1908, grey schist.

Photographed by Ren Chao

降魔，2~3 世纪，马尔丹收集，
白沙瓦博物馆，藏品号 2765

摄影 任超

Mara's attack, 2nd-3rd century, received from Mardan Guides Mess,
Peshawar Museum, No. 2765.

Photographed by Ren Chao

降魔，2~3 世纪，1950 年收购，
白沙瓦博物馆，藏品号 2766

摄影 任超

Mara's attack, 2nd-3rd century, purchased in 1950,
Peshawar Museum, No. 2766.

Photographed by Ren Chao

降魔，2~3 世纪，萨合力巴洛尔 1906~1907 年发掘，片岩
白沙瓦博物馆，藏品号 2767

摄影 任超

Mara's attack, 2nd-3rd century, Sahri Bahlol, exc. 1906-1907, schist
Peshawar Museum, No. 2767.

Photographed by Ren Chao

降魔，2~3 世纪，
白沙瓦博物馆，藏品号 2768

摄影 任超

Mara's attack, 2nd-3rd century,
Peshawar Museum, No. 2768.

Photographed by Ren Chao

二商人奉食，2~3 世纪，马尔丹收集，1912 年收购，
白沙瓦博物馆，藏品号 2775

摄影 任超

Two merchants offering food, 2nd-3rd century, Mardan, purchased in 1912,
Peshawar Museum, No. 2775.

Photographed by Ren Chao

四天王奉钵，2~3 世纪，萨合力巴洛尔 1911~1912 年发掘，片岩，
白沙瓦博物馆，藏品号 2774

摄影 任超

*Offering of four bowls, 2nd-3rd century, Sahri Bahlol,
exc. 1911~1912, schist, Peshawar Museum, No. 2774.*

Photographed by Ren Chao

天神劝请，2~3 世纪，巴利科特，捐赠，
白沙瓦博物馆，藏品号 2776

摄影 任超

*Gods entreat the Buddha to preach, 2nd-3rd century, Barikot
Swat, donation, Peshawar Museum, No. 2776.*

Photographed by Ren Chao

天神劝请，2~3 世纪，捐赠，
白沙瓦博物馆，藏品号 2777

摄影 任超

Gods entreat the Buddha to preach, 2nd-3rd century, donation,
Peshawar Museum, No. 2777.

Photographed by Ren Chao

初转法轮，2~3 世纪，萨合力巴洛尔 1906-1907 年发掘，片岩，
白沙瓦博物馆，藏品号 2781

摄影 范晶晶

The first sermon, 2nd-3rd century, Sahri Bahlol, exc. 1906-1907,
Peshawar Museum, No. 2781.

Photographed by Fan Jingjing

犍陀罗的微笑 巴基斯坦古迹文物巡礼

初转法轮，2~3 世纪，马尔丹收集，
白沙瓦博物馆，藏品号 2782

摄影 任超

The first sermon, 2nd-3rd century, received from Mardan Guides Mess,
Peshawar Museum, No. 2782.

Photographed by Ren Chao

舍卫城神变，2~3 世纪，萨合力巴洛尔 1911~1912 年发掘，片岩，
白沙瓦博物馆，藏品号 2771

摄影 任超

The miracle at Sravasti, 2nd-3rd century, Sahri Bahlol, exc. 1911-1912, schist,
Peshawar Museum, No. 2771.

Photographed by Ren Chao

佛陀神变, 2~3 世纪,
达赫德巴依 1912 年发掘,
白沙瓦博物馆, 藏品号 2786

摄影 任超

The miracle of Buddha transforming into different
images, 2nd-3rd century, Takht-i-Bahi, exc. 1912,
Peshawar Museum, No. 2786.

Photographed by Ren Chao

犍陀罗的微笑

巴基斯坦古迹文物巡礼

佛自三十三天下，2~3 世纪，
白沙瓦博物馆，藏品号 2788

摄影 范晶晶

The Buddha descending from Trayastrimsa heaven, 2nd-3rd century,
Peshawar Museum, No. 2788.

Photographed by Fan Jingjing

帝释访佛，2~3世纪，玛玛内，1928年收购，
白沙瓦博物馆，藏品号 2805

摄影 任超

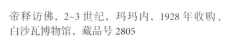

Visit of Indra to the Buddha, 2nd-3rd century,
Mamane Dheri, purchased in 1928,
Peshawar Museum, No. 2805.

Photographed by Ren Chao

帝释访佛，基利，千枚岩，
塔克西拉博物馆

摄影 范晶晶

Visit of Indra to the Buddha, Giri, phyllite,
Taxila Museum.

Photographed by Fan Jingjing

涅槃，2~3 世纪，萨合力巴洛尔 1906~1907 年发掘，片岩，
白沙瓦博物馆，藏品号 2826

摄影　任超

Nirvana scene, 2nd-3rd century, Sahri Bahlol, exc. 1906-1907, schist,
Peshawar Museum, No. 2826.

Photographed by Ren Chao

涅槃，2~3 世纪，萨合力巴洛尔 1906~1907 年发掘，片岩，
白沙瓦博物馆，藏品号 2827

摄影　任超

Nirvana scene, 2nd-3rd century, Sahri Bahlol, exc. 1906-1907, schist,
Peshawar Museum, No. 2827.

Photographed by Ren Chao

茶毗，2~3 世纪，捐赠，
白沙瓦博物馆，藏品号 2833

摄影 范晶晶

Cremation of the Buddha, 2nd-3rd century, donation,
Peshawar Museum, No. 2833.

Photographed by Fan Jingjing

分舍利，2~3 世纪，1934 年收购，
白沙瓦博物馆，藏品号 2831

摄影 范晶晶

Distribution of the relics, 2nd-3rd century, purchased in 1934,
Peshawar Museum, No. 2831.

Photographed by Fan Jingjing

初转法轮，难陀出家，提婆达多害佛，
涅槃（从上至下），2~3 世纪，
达赫德巴依 1912 年发掘，
白沙瓦博物馆，藏品号 2822

摄影 任超

First sermon, Nanda's conversion, Devadatta's
scheme, nirvana scene(from top to bottom),
2nd -3rd century,
Takht-i-Bahi, exc. 1912,
Peshawar Museum, No. 2822.

Photographed by Ren Chao

犍
陀
罗
的
微
笑

巴
基
斯
坦
古
迹
文
物
巡
礼

HARITI AND PANCIKA

诃利帝与般支迦

Hariti is well known as "Mother of Ghost Children" in Chinese Buddhist literature. She was certainly one of the earliest goddesses to have been widely worshipped in the Indian Buddhist world. According to the mythic story as told by *Sarvastivadins*, goddess Hariti was born as the daughter of a *yaksa* in charge of protection of a capital city. Her husband, the *yaksa* Pancika, was native in Gandhara region. Hariti was first regarded as a dreadful evil deity who used to snatch the children from human world and devour them. It was Buddha who converted Hariti to a supportive goddess by hiding one of her 500 children so that she could experience a similiar anxiety and distress of mothers who had lost their children due to Hariti's evil habituation. Because of Buddha's influence, Hariti gave up her evil ways and became a faithful guardian goddess of the Buddhism while taking charge of protecting children from diseases.

It is quite certain to say the worship to goddess Hariti was popular and related to the development of Buddhism in Gandhara region since very early time. Even later in the first half of the 7th century, when Xuan Zang arrived in Gandhara, he noticed that there was a stupa erected at the spot where Hariti had been converted by the Buddha. About a half century later, *The Record of the Buddhist Religion as practiced in Indian and Malay Archipelogo* by I-Tsing—the name of the famous Chinese author as translated by the Japanese scholar Takadusu, described in detail how Hariti was worshipped by Indian Buddhist laymen with food offerings. From Gandhara the worship to Mother goddess Hariti was widely spread within the Buddhist world even beyond South Asia. Her figure can also be found in Southeast Asia; with the Buddhism coming to the east, she was also worshipped as a wish granting deity in several areas of China and in Japan.

Nowadays, specimens of Hariti can be seen in many museums in the world. In Peshwar museum we see several statues of Hariti in company with or without her husband Pancika.

Duan Qing

诃利帝，在汉文佛教文献中又称"鬼子母"。这一神灵的形象似乎是伴随着佛教的发展而产生的。依据说一切有部的记载，诃利帝是护城夜叉之女，她的丈夫般支迦是犍陀罗地的夜叉。她初为恶神，自己生育了五百个孩子，却喜噉食人间小儿。后来经过佛陀的感化而皈依佛法，抑恶从善，成为关心小儿疾苦、爱护小儿的护法神。

尤其在犍陀罗地区，这尊神灵与佛教有不解之缘，曾经分享佛、菩萨的供奉。据《大唐西域记》记载，佛陀释迦牟尼点化"鬼子母"的窣堵波就在犍陀罗国。依据《南海寄归内法传》，在 7 世纪末 8 世纪初的印度仍然有供养"鬼子母"的习俗。还应提及，在犍陀罗以外地区，对诃利帝的信仰之流传也颇为广泛。无论在南亚次大陆，在东南亚，还是沿佛教东渐的路径进入中国，乃至日本，凡是有佛教曾经流行之地，就能找到她的形象。

犍陀罗地区出土的诃利帝的造像有些已经入藏全球多家博物馆。而在巴基斯坦各博物馆，仍至少收藏有 6 尊诃利帝的造像。我们在白沙瓦博物馆可以看到多件"诃利帝"像，多数有她的丈夫般支迦的陪伴。

段晴

诃利帝造像，公元2~3 世纪，萨合力巴洛尔 1911~1912 年发掘，片岩
白沙瓦博物馆

摄影 任超

Hariti, 2nd-3rd century,
excavated from Sahri Bahlol during 1911-1912, grey schist,
Peshawar Museum.

Photographed by Ren Chao

般支迦与诃利帝，公元 2~3 世纪，
沙吉基台利 1909~1910 年发掘，片岩，
白沙瓦博物馆

摄影 孟嗣徽

Pancika and Hariti, Grey schist, 2nd-
3rd century, excavated from Shah-ji-ki-
Dheri during 1911-1912,
Peshawar Museum.

Photographed by Meng Sihui

THE RELIQUARY

舍利盒

The bronze, once gilded reliquary of Peshawar Museum is always designated as "Kanishka casket" since its discovery in 1908 at the site Shah-ji-ki-Dheri from the ruined monument which is positively identified as the legendary stupa erected by the Kushan king Kanishka. Since then, much has been disputed and argued about the images and designs on the casket, and about Kharosthi texts which are dotted on it. A breakthrough has been achieved in 2002 when Errington and Falk published their results of research: it is not a casket of Kanishka, but one made in time when his successor Huvishka was on the throne, which is donated by two architects of the fire-hall in the monastery founded by (Mahārā)ja Kanishka, and was accepted by *ācāryas* of the school *Sarvastivadins* (Elizabeth Errington, "Numismatic evidence for dating the 'Kaniṣka' reliquary"; Harry Falk, "Appendix: The inscription on the so-called Kaniṣka casket" *Silk Road Art and Archaeology* (S. R. A. A.) VIII, 101-115).

Duan Qing

白沙瓦博物馆的著名珍宝之一，是一件铜制的舍利盒，外面曾经有一层镀金，但已经看不出来了。1908 年，考古学家对沙吉基台利遗址进行发掘时，从佛塔废墟中出土了这件舍利盒。这座佛塔，据说正是如《大唐西域记》所记载的具有传奇色彩的大塔，为迦腻色伽王所建造。一个世纪以来，众学者争论不休，针对这舍利盒上的图案以及点缀而成的几行佉卢文的释读，各抒己见。2002 年英国博物馆的学者艾琳童联合德国柏林印度学著名教授法尔科发表了他们的研究成果，取得了突破性的进展。他们认为，这件舍利盒并非是"迦腻色伽王"的舍利盒，因为放进塔里的时间当在迦腻色伽王的继承者胡毗色伽王在世的时候。供养舍利盒的是一所寺院的火厅的两位设计师，接收这舍利盒的是说一切有部的法师。而那座寺院，确实是迦腻色伽王所建造。这些都以佉卢文明确地记载在这舍利盒上。

段晴

舍利盒，公元 2 世纪，
贵霜王胡毗色伽时代造，铜鎏金
白沙瓦博物馆

摄 影 任 超

A gilded bronze reliquary from the time of
Huvishka's reign (153-191A.D.),
Peshawar Museum.

Photographed by Ren Chao

舍利盒盖，中间为佛坐像，右为因陀罗像，
左为梵天像

摄影 任超

On the lid, in the middle, Buddha Shakyamuni is seated in
abhaya mudra on an inverted lotus, flanked by Indra on the
right and Brahmā on the left.

Photographed by Ren Chao

GANDHARA'S SMILE
THE TOUR OF CULTURAL RELICS IN PAKISTAN

03
———

EPILOGUE

结语

Our trip had a small mission: to walk in today's Pakistan, to see the history and culture of thousands of years, to feel the diversity of civilizations, to understand the gentleness and inclusiveness under the sharp edges.

We hope that the advanced technology, convenient transportation and developed communications in modern times should not bring us to a rashness of a superfacial judgment. We grow up and develop in different regions, experience peace and war, glory and loss. Let us appreciate each other's beauty for a joint future. Let us recognize each other's differences and respect each other on the road ahead. Although we are different, we have the same expectation for the future.

This book is dedicated to our dearest friend—Pakistan.

Zhang Jiamei

行走在今日的巴基斯坦，看千年的历史文化，感受文明中丰富多彩的多元交叉，去理解棱角分明下的温和与包容。

希望当代先进的科技、便利的交通、发达的通信，不要成为我们轻易评判别人的工具。我们各自在不同的地域上成长、发展；经历合作、战争；体味荣耀、彷徨。让我们欣赏彼此的美，认识彼此的不同，融入彼此的未来。在今后的道路上，保持相互的尊重。虽然我们不一样，但对未来，也许，我们有共同的向往。

谨以此书，献给最可爱的巴基斯坦朋友。

张嘉妹

楗陀罗的微笑 —— 巴基斯坦古迹文物巡礼

图书在版编目（ＣＩＰ）数据

犍陀罗的微笑：巴基斯坦古迹文物巡礼 / 张嘉妹主编 . -- 上海 ：上海三联书店，2021.1

ISBN 978-7-5426-7246-9

Ⅰ.①犍… Ⅱ.①张… Ⅲ.①名胜古迹 – 介绍 – 巴基斯坦②历史文物 – 介绍 – 巴基斯坦 Ⅳ.① K935.37

中国版本图书馆 CIP 数据核字 (2020) 第 216524 号

犍陀罗的微笑　巴基斯坦古迹文物巡礼

主　编：张嘉妹	责任编辑：黄 韬	装帧设计：覃一彪	监　制：姚 军	责任校对：张大伟　王凌霄	

出版发行 上海三联书店 （200030） 中国上海市漕溪北路 331 号 A 座 6 楼　　邮购电话：021-22895540

印　刷：上海南朝印刷有限公司　　版　次：2021 年 1 月第 1 版　　印　次：2021 年 1 月第 1 次印刷

开　本：889mm × 1194mm 1/12　　字　数：100 千字　　印　张：12

书　号：ISBN 978-7-5426-7246-9/K·618　　定　价：168 元

* 敬启读者，如发现本书有印装质量问题，请与印刷厂联系 021-62213990